Girdled and Gloved is a memoir that reads like a novel or a case history. It's a humorous and poignant mother-daughter story of riding streetcars in Atlanta, enduring blackouts, collecting tin foil during World War II, selling shoes at Rich's Department Store in the 50s, singing on live TV, majoring in drama, failing auditions, marriage, and psychotherapy. The story that asks, "Can this child rise above her circumstances and create her own American Dream in the girdled and gloved 50s?" Then stay tuned for the amazing epilogue: *From Radio to YouTube!*

"A Southern storyteller captures an era with humor, pathos, and insight."

WHAT READERS ARE SAYING

"From beginning to end, this is the most original memoir I've ever read."
"This is an excellent memoir. I wouldn't know what memoir to compare it with, but it certainly stands on its own."
"The right amount of vulnerability, humor and self-revelation."
"The writing is so rich and descriptive with an amazing memory for details."
"Love the fads, foods and feelings—an original account of the 40s and 50s. Great descriptions. Would make an interesting movie!"
"Beautiful reflective passages that read like melting chocolate."

Girdled
and
Gloved

From Radio to YouTube

Charlotte Ashurst McDaniel

Acknowledgments

Girdled & Gloved: From Radio to YouTube
is a work of creative non fiction.
Some names have been changed.

Cover photo: Author's collection
(l-r, Charlotte Ashurst, Sandra Brown, Frances Witherspoon, Kay Tallant,)

Death notice, 1929, courtesy of *The Atlanta Journal*
University of Georgia Pandora Yearbook 1958-59 photos.

Thanks to:
Gotham Writers Workshop
OLLI@UGa Memoir Writing Group
Hannelore Hahn, founder of
International Women Writers Guild (IWWG)
Editorial assistants and readers:
Dr. Althea Ashe, Regina Anderson Lucas
Phyllis Howling, Mary Padgelek, Susan Svenson,
Katy Terry, Sarah Upshaw Vaughn, Val Mathews
Typists: Lee Feather, Bowen Craig
Special thanks to: Evaluator Ron

~

Copyright © 2016 Charlotte Ashurst McDaniel

All rights reserved.

ISBN-10:1534801278
ISBN-13:978-1534801271

CONTENTS

Preface

PROLOGUE

1. In the Beginning 1
2. The House in Black and White 8
3. School Days - Piano Lessons and WWII 14
4. My Father's Hobby Was the Dictionary 26
5. Riding the Streetcar with Evelyn Keyes 33
6. By Hook or By Crook 40
7. Radio Days and Movie Stars 50
8. Socializing the Heathen 59
9. The Holy Washrag 73
10. The King of Hearts 82
11. Eighth Grade Madness 93
12. The Discovery and the Dawning Reality 101
13. "Don't Call Us, We'll Call You!" 107
14. I Need a Little Magic 126
15. '49 Ford with Twin Smitties 135
16. The Drama of a Drama Major 149
17. Into the Mainstream 162
18. Hold onto Your Dreams 171
19. Betty Crocker Is Not Allowed to Scream! 179
20. "Vy Are You Here?" 190

EPILOGUE

From Radio to YouTube 200

Preface

We all share the journey of growing up, overcoming obstacles, giving up childish ways, then leaving home to go into the world to seek our fortunes. In writing this book I was searching for my own turning points, wondering if I ever had any choices at all, up until age twenty-one. For it seemed to me as if my life *lived me*, shaping me within the context of Atlanta, the family I was born into, and the gloved and girdled generation I grew up in.

I wanted to tell what it was like to grow up in Atlanta during the time of streetcars, remembering the dusty playground of Joel Chandler Harris Grammar School where soldiers from Fort McPherson gave bouncy jeep rides to school children during World War II. I wanted to recreate the experience of listening to the radio, collecting movie star photos, and the exhilaration of riding a bicycle to the Saturday movies.

I wanted to paint a portrait of living Mother's dreams in a world of bobby pins, movies, baptism, fresh peaches, kudzu, Peachtree Street, and the University of Georgia.

Until I wrote this memoir I had hardly realized, much less appreciated, Mother's getting me through college on an office clerk's salary.

I believe that every life is unique and precious, and that a story not recorded is lost forever, so in 1991 I plunged in and began this story to see what I might remember.

Writing, creating music, and dreamwork have helped me understand how my early years influenced my life journey. Over the twenty-five years it's taken me to complete this book, I've gained insight, adding nuances, and poetic commentary.

Finally, an epilogue emerged that surprised even me.

At best, I have developed more compassion for the forces of nature and nurture, so that I might have that "happy ending" I longed for—for I have come to believe in the grace that comes from understanding and accepting the past.

Charlotte Ashurst McDaniel

PROLOGUE

AFTER THREE MONTHS OF MARRIAGE in our little garage apartment, I just lost it. I crumpled up on the sofa with those ill-fitting floral slipcovers, and cried in hysterics. With tears still streaming down my face, I picked up my ukelele and strummed the chords to "Show Me the Way to Go Home."

It was 1958. I was twenty-two.

The next morning, I left my young husband.

After six weeks of estrangement, he suggested we go for marriage counseling. Dressed in my navy-blue "going-away" suit and matching high heel pumps, I met him at Family Counseling in an old renovated house. In a tall dark room, we sat across from a woman interviewer behind a large imposing desk.

"Why have you come for counseling?" she asked.

My husband pulled out a long yellow legal pad from his heavy briefcase, adjusted his horn-rimmed glasses, and read from an itemized list.

Ho-ly Cow! I thought, glancing sideways at his business-like approach. I cringed, slumping in my chair, scraping at my ragged thumbnail scar, hearing a litany of the errors of my ways. I felt humiliated to be so judged and exposed in front of a stranger, no less. Next, he read a list of reasons for continuing the marriage.

I don't remember a single item on that list.

The interviewer looked at me.

If I'd had any awareness of my situation, I would've said, *Look, seven months ago I was onstage playing Elizabeth in* The Circle. *I was a valued human being, and now I'm feeling like an utter failure, and no one seems to understand.*

But when my turn came, I said I didn't know if I really *did* want to get back together, but since *I'd* left the marriage, there must be something wrong with *me,* and so I should at least try to find out what it was—and why.

Mrs. Millie Keeler, my counselor, turned out to be a godsend. She was short and jolly—someone I could talk to for the first time in my life. She joked me out of all my apprehensions. In a few weeks my husband and I got back together. I even lightened up a little and didn't hold everything inside because I knew I'd have Mrs. Keeler to talk to in my next session—to freely tell what *I'd said* and what *he'd said.*

Then after a December session, when I'd humorously described decorating our first Christmas tree, she looked at me squarely and said, "Beginning in January, you are to see a psychiatrist."

Oh, Lord, what is wrong with me? I wondered.

~

When I was in third grade I overheard Mrs. Callaway say, "Charlotte's voice isn't good enough." That's when I started being like someone in the movies . . . anyone but me.

Chapter 1

In the Beginning

(My Fourth birthday)

FOR THIRTEEN YEARS MOTHER AND I SLEPT in a double bed shoved up next to the outside wall of an enclosed backporch leaving us about a foot of room to walk by. Everyday she left me with Grandma and took the streetcar to downtown Atlanta to operate an address-o-graph machine at Rich's Department Store.

I wish I had a better story to tell you. I wish I'd been born to more high-minded people with books and manners, and nicer furniture. But in 1937, when I was eight months old, Mother and my father divorced, and she brought me back to live in the house she grew up in. I was a real imposition on Grandma because she'd already had enough tragedy in her life.

So, I'll start by saying that my story is more about being *born* with a broken heart than anything else. I know it's hard to think that a baby could come out of a womb so sad and all, but I did. Embedded in me from the beginning was a sense of loss. We weren't a real family, just a threesome of survivors—Grandma, Mother and me.

Maybe that's why I silently dreamed of doing something so big I'd always be remembered.

~

My first memory is of bright morning sunlight casting a pattern of black and white shadows from my playpen onto the porch of 421 Holderness Street—the house I am to live in for twenty-one years. I'm looking through wooden bars, past the banisters, across a low privet hedge, to the porch next door. I see James Alden kneeling on one knee, in tan knickers, as he carefully stacks up his blocks, building castles with turrets, higher and higher. He looks over at me with his serious brown eyes, his brown hair falling over an earnest face.

"Watch this, Charlotte," he says with a soft smile.

With one gentle touch, he topples them over. I jump up and down, rattling my playpen rail with the red and blue wooden beads strung on a wire crosspiece. I see a flicker of wispy blond hair catching the sunlight.

FAMILY SECRETS AND MYSTERIES

I think our first memories tell us something about both the nature and nurture we have been born into, and even more about *how* we will learn to cope with our circumstances.

In my case, as this may turn out to be, I would say that being alone, but safely cooped up, is formative. I will learn to "make do" and content myself with whatever is around me, while imagining a world where the porch is my stage and the passersby my audience. I would say this situation will be pretty symbolic of my life to come—that, and noticing light and shadow.

What I hadn't realized was that even *before* my birth in 1936, an indelible stream of events was *already* connected to me, flowing through the veins of a tragic family history.

In my case, the family story handed down was that Sherman's troops stormed right up to the old homeplace on Jett Road in Cobb County, near Atlanta, where Grandma's family had buried their food in the root cellar, *'but the Yankees found it and took ever' last bit!'*

Grandma told me this from her rocker by the coal stove.

My great-great-grandfather rode in the cavalry for the Confederacy. Engraved on his tombstone in Mt. Paran Baptist Church Cemetery:

Seaborn Jones,
Lost an Arm in The Battle of Manassas

"When they sawed off his arm, they jis' flung it out the window," Grandma said without flinching.

~

In 1903, Grandma, born Ola Jane Jones, the youngest of six, stuffed a few clothes in a croker sack, and set out walking through the fields and onto a dusty, red dirt road where she hitched a ride in a wagon to the end of the streetcar line leading into the fast growing city of Atlanta. She was lured by the clang of streetcars, city lights, nickelodeons—a better life in a house with indoor plumbing, like her married sister, Alice, had.

Ola Jane met a jolly streetcar conductor who hailed from North Georgia, Arthur C. Chappelear, called *Chap*. They married in 1905 and had two girls: Gladys, in 1907 and my mother, Margaret, born in 1909.

Everyone called Mother *Totsy*.

~

Tragedy struck when their house on Rankin Street burned to the ground during one of the worst fires in Atlanta destroying dozens of neighborhoods in the Boulevard area.

The newspaper in Atlanta said, *'Only Sherman's fire in 1864 did more damage.'*

(Arthur C. and Ola Chappelear c. 1910)

After that disaster my grandparents bought a house on Holderness Street in the West End section of Atlanta. Mother and Aunt Gladys went to Lee Street School. Then in 1929, another tragedy happened when my grandmother was in a car wreck that led to my grandfather's death.

The more I learned about that story, the more I thought my family was fated right from the start.

I pieced together this story: In August 1929, Grandma was in her brother Oscar's car headed off to Florida with some of his cronies. (He was a construction supervisor.) They had a wreck at the Lee Street underpass. Grandma was crushed in the back seat, with a broken pelvis and leg.

My grandfather went to see her in Piedmont Hospital and was so upset he rushed home and called his friend, Harry Poole, who was a mortician in the funeral business.

"Harry, you're going to get an ambulance call soon, take care of it yourself," he said.

Then my grandfather went out in the front yard on Holderness Street and put a bullet through his head.

~

The Atlanta Journal carried this headline:

WORRIED OVER WIFE'S INJURY, MAN SUICIDES

Arthur Chappelear, Power Company Veteran, Fires Bullet Into Brain

---

A. C. Chappelear, ill and worried over
the condition of his wife,
who is in a hospital suffering injuries
from a motor car accident last Saturday,
shot and killed himself in the front yard.
At the hospital, it was said that Mrs. Chappelear
was suffering with a fractured hip
and fractured right leg.
She was not informed of her husband's death.

Mother was twenty. She never told me anything about her father's death.

~

LIVING MOTHER'S DREAMS

(Mother, c. 1940 age 31)

Mother had greenish eyes, a ruddy complexion, dark wavy hair, medium oily skin, beautiful teeth, and a pretty smile, of which she was very proud. She wore rimless glasses, a little pressed powder and *Tangee* lip rouge, which she put on with her little finger.

Every Sunday afternoon, Mother and I walked over a mile to see whatever was playing at the Gordon Theater in West End. Sitting next to Mother I felt such strong passions from all those

larger than life images on the silver screen as if I was attached by an umbilical of emotions.

I saw so many movies that every frame of reference for my life literally came from the *frame* of a movie reel.

Mother loved to pose me for pictures. She put me on the porch in my pajamas holding her old straw-filled teddy bear. She placed a rubber toy figure of Popeye on a table to capture his shadow on the clapboard siding.

When my hair grew down to my waist, she posed me by the fish pond with my hands clasped angelically like a child in a Silent Movie. I was her little movie star. Those photos were tucked away in the silk purse of my silent dreams.

~

Mother was seventy-five when I finally got up enough nerve to ask questions about her father's death. She was in a nursing home with a broken hip and diabetes, I brought her some azaleas, sugar-free Certs, and bananas that day.

She took the bananas saying, "Good, Shug, two green and two ripe." Then she leaned over and tucked them in her metal bedside table among balls of rolled-up white socks.

I said, as matter-of-factly as I could, "Mother, why do you think your father shot himself?"

Undaunted, she replied, "Well, I never thought much about it. Like I said, Papa was upset over Mama being in the hospital, and if he wanted to just go out and shoot himself, well, he did."

"Geezus!" I thought, *I'll never know because Aunt Gladys is already dead.*

I decided to ask about Mother's mysterious first marriage, since I'd found a divorce decree rumaging in the family trunk at fourteen. She'd never told me about that either.

"Tell me about you and Walter Gray."

"Walter Gray?" she replied raising her eyebrows like, *how do you know about him?* She shifted gears into her "story-telling" voice.

"Well, we married and then we separated, and he left and went on to Nawth Carolina. And just before the divorce was final, he slit his throat with a knife."

That's just how she said it: *"Slit his throat with a knife!"*

She even swiped her arthritic finger across her neck like a movie director.

"So-o-o-o," she continued, caught up in her tale, "when people asked me what happened to my first husband, I usta' say, *'He died of a throat condition!'*"

She laughed in delight at her perfect punch line.

Later I learned that my cousins, Sonny and Susan, were told by Aunt Gladys that their grandfather had *'died at a picnic from eating a black walnut pie that had too much sugar in it!'*

~

Mother used to sing, "I Get the Blues When It Rains." When I hear that song, I start wondering again about her early life in the Jazz Age, yet I know I'll never know who she was, or the whole story. But then, we never know what our parents are really like, do we?

Maybe it's better that way.

(Mother's friend, Grace and Mother, double-dating in the N. Georgia Mountains. c.1928)

Chapter 2

The House in Black and White

I WAS BORN AND BRED IN A CULTURE that was uniquely Southern in its irrational fits and starts of hypocrisy, sinners, and Yankees. Our Southern Baptist Church could take on a spell of joyous wildness during the week of a summer revival. Monday night: *Hallelujah!* Tuesday night: *Thine the Glory!* Wednesday night: *Revive Us Again!* As if, having re-dedicated our life to Jesus and been *revived*, we could all go back to the way the South had once been. And especially not have to remember defeat.

Much of my life has escaped me. Yet in that dark theater of my memory, the rooms of the house remain mysteriously vivid.

Grandma rented one side of her house to a string of tenants who shared our front porch rockers. The small dark living room parlor was partitioned off with heavy sliding doors. The fireplace cemented over, and a gas radiant heater sat on a bilious green tiled hearth.

Over the mantle loomed a framed picture of a ship in a storm. That painting within its dark, dusty, ornate frame, with the moonlight on the waves and the ship struggling against the forces of nature—that's what Mother and Grandma felt like, to me. It seemed as if they, too, were stuck in a framework of time past, because everything in that dark house just got older or broken—a patched-up roof, a sagging garage, wobbly tables, and peeling wallpaper.

Ironically, it was under that dark painting that hope arrived each year, because I hung up one of Mother's rayon stockings on a nail under the mantle.

I tried to stay awake under a layer of quilts, listening for the jingles of those reindeer parked on our scruffy little front yard. I figured Santa had to come in the front door, because the fireplaces were cemented over.

I always woke up early on Christmas morning.

"Wait here Shug," Mother would say, shivering, putting on her robe, then padding up the cold hallway to light the heater and let it warm up for five long minutes. I could barely wait to run up the dark hallway. Mother would've plugged in the Christmas tree lights, and a new toy would be there waiting for me. One year I was overjoyed to find a tiny wind-up train that went around on a circular track.

Another year a war bond was rolled up, sticking out the top of Mother's stocking. I didn't care at all about a war bond, but I knew it was important to Mother and Grandma because they, like everyone else, wanted to do their part during the war.

The young child *me* was happy just to get an orange, an apple, a peppermint cane, some mixed nuts, and a new toy. Grandma would come in later, wrapped in her flannel robe after she'd had her favorite cup of Eight O'Clock coffee. There were no exciting presents for them—maybe a pair of gloves or stockings, but no fox fur, like in the movies—or a satin dress.

The best present I ever had, though, was my blue bicycle. I'd already picked it out at Western Auto, but it was finally mine to ride on Christmas Day.

After the bicycle, nothing was ever as special, but I kept expecting it to be, and from then on, there was always an edge of disappointment. I spent so much of my teenage years looking for lost love under a Christmas tree.

As I describe that house, I'm struck by how beautiful it must've been when Mother first moved there in fourth grade, back in 1918.

In that tiny, cold, living-room parlor there was still a handsome floor radio that crackled static whenever I turned it on. My grandfather probably bought it back in the 20s, along with the wrought iron maroon velour radio bench—the one that wound up in our little backporch bedroom.

I've imagined that when Mother was twelve and her sister Gladys, fourteen, they celebrated Christmas right there with the sliding doors open, making the room much larger. Maybe they gathered around a warm fire in the fireplace, like a real family. And perhaps they each got a locket and presents from Grandma's five brothers and sisters.

Anyway, that's how I'd like to think it was back in 1921, say.

Gradually Grandma's dark house would become as familiar as the spiders that lay dead in their cobweb coffins. I remember the gritty window sills I rested my elbows on and the furry coating of dust that hung on the heavy mantles. It was as if all the family secrets were sealed away in those cemented-over fireplaces.

THE NEXT-DOOR NEIGHBORS

The Aldens lived next door in a small brick duplex squeezed in on the corner lot. Their kitchen screen-door faced our kitchen window, with the hedge in between. In summer we overheard the Alden's arguments.

Once I heard Grandma say to her sister Alice on the phone, "Mitch Alden is a drunkard!"

Mr. Alden sold encyclopedias and stayed home a lot. Mrs. Alden wore dark suits and a dark hat pulled down at an angle over thick glasses. She took the streetcar to her job downtown and left an old black Buick for Mr. Alden.

Their son, James—the boy who stacked up blocks—died at thirteen. I was too young to remember his death, but sometimes I'd hear Mother and Grandma mention James Alden, and I'd say, "Where's James?"

"James died," Mother would say, and once added, "Oh-h-h, James *lov-ed you.*"

I can still feel the melting warmth in Mother's voice that day.

Grandma said James Alden died of a cerebral hemorrhage and yelled at me every time I stood on my head. "STOP THAT!! The blood'll rush to your head, and you'll die just like James!"

Everyone could remember James, sort of like Jesus. Just to know someone really loved me brought more comfort than Sunday School teachers telling me Jesus loved me.

Jesus never met me. James had.

My first memory of the Alden's younger child, Lucy, was watching her unfold her doll's wardrobe on that same porch which had no railing. The doll's trunk opened like a thick book into a magical closet. She took tiny dresses off little hangers and put them on her doll—one that had real-looking hair. Then she placed a little wide-brimmed straw hat on the doll's head and tied a tiny ribbon under its doll chin.

What Heaven! There was Lucy and her dolls—twenty feet away—but as different as night and day from life in Grandma's dark house.

Lucy wore pretty dresses and a ribbon in her dark brown hair. I even imagined those toys were things Shirley Temple might have had in her Hollywood home.

Occasionally I was allowed to visit Lucy and we played card games on their colorful hook rug. I loved the small bookcase in the living room where Lucy stored her boxed set of miniature cards, every bit as wonderful as the doll's wardrobe. We would sit on the floor and Lucy would deal out the tiny cards and teach me how to play *Old Maid* or *Go Fish*.

How wonderful to have an older girl to laugh with at *Slap Jack*. And what magic to see her bed with an organdy canopy top, a little boudoir table with a glass top, an oval mirror, and a pink organdy skirt. The curved boudoir table had tiny folding arms that pulled out, revealing a secret drawer where Lucy kept her hair ribbons and barrettes.

My visits to play with Lucy were when Mr. Alden was home in the summer, when Mrs. Alden was at work. I remember that once, while we were in the living room playing *Go Fish*, Mr. Alden called from the back hallway, "Lucy, could you bring me some soap?" He was apparently in the bathroom. For some reason, I walked to the entranceway to the hall, and just at that moment, Mr. Alden opened the door, so that I saw him naked.

Was it deliberate?

Now that I'm writing and remembering, I feel strangely disturbed by it all—things I've repressed, perhaps. And now I'm wondering about James's death at thirteen from a cerebral hemorrhage from "standing on his head."

And then came that horrible, unforgettable day when Grandma said, "You are never to speak to Lucy or any of them Aldens again. DO YOU HEAR, ME?"

I was only about four or five. It scared me to hear Grandma's ferocious voice like a protective bear. I didn't know what to think.

That night Mother looked stern and said the same thing.

"Shug, you are never *ever* to speak to Lucy again," thus confirming the pronouncement.

Maybe I had "acted funny" and Grandma or Mother had wrangled the truth out of me the day I saw Mr. Alden naked.

And if that's so, look what the truth got me: banishment from a magic kingdom.

I remember that I sucked my fingers and cried for days, almost unable to breathe from the suffocation of that separation from Lucy's world. The reminder of the banishment was always there, like a curse, or a horrible spell had been cast upon me, as if a piece of my heart had been cut out and my tongue, too.

For a long time I thought it was all my fault because earlier I had sat on Lucy's violin bow lying on their sofa and cracked it. Mrs. Alden was furious, and Mother had to pay four dollars for a new one. I was so ashamed. Whatever they had discovered I never knew, but I was a good little girl, so I shut my mouth, locked it, and threw away the key.

I never spoke to any of them again. The spell would never be lifted, leaving an unquenchable ache and longing over any separation—ever after—as they say in fairy tales.

Year after year, if I heard Lucy coming out the door, I ducked my head and silently watched from under shaded eyes, or peered from behind the front door screen, my heart bursting to beat again with devotion. I watched Lucy in pleated skirts and sweaters carrying her books to high school. Later Mother said Lucy was voted best-dressed girl at Wesleyan College in Macon, Georgia.

~

The few books we owned gathered dust on the mantle in Grandma's dark bedroom: *Lamb in His Bosom*, *The Shore Dimly Seen,* and the one I remember best, a large commemorative edition of *Gone with the Wind*, bought by thousands of Atlantans in 1939 when Clark Gable came to the premier at the Loew's Grand.

I remember someone would fetch it down. I loved looking at the beautiful 8 x 10 glossy color photos, especially Scarlett with rosy cheeks, red lips, wearing a frothy white dress with green flowers. She was at the Wilkes' barbecue. Beaus were kneeling at her feet vying to bring her scrumptious desserts out on the elegantly wide steps. Oh, those beautiful glimpses of a technicolor world inside my black-and-white house.

Who wouldn't want to live like that? I thought.

The house at 421 Holderness Street was already filled with shame, sadness, defeat, and resignation. So, it's no wonder music and the movies would become important for shaping and escaping.

~

Chapter 3

School – Piano Lessons and WW II

I'M TOLD I SAT ON THE FRONT STEPS asking the passing children, *"Goin' t'kool? Goin' t'kool?"*

In August before entering school Mother and I stood in a long line with other mothers and children waiting to get a smallpox vaccination and visit our class. I got my shot on my leg. Soon a big red itchy scab formed, the size of a half-a-dollar. Everyone said, 'don't pick at it,' but of course I did.

That first day of school Grandma and I walked five blocks down Lucille Avenue passing over a railroad overpass just before my beautiful brick school building, J. C. Harris.

"Bye, Grandma," I said, right there on the sidewalk, "I know how to get back home." Then I turned and skipped past the American Flag with its clanking lanyards, trekked up the wide front school steps, into the long hallway, and down the wide marble steps to Mrs. Lyle's Kindergarten class.

Here was a big romantic technicolor world waiting just for me. I took ownership immediately. There were more toys than I'd ever seen, a French-paned door leading outside, and sunny windows from which I watched the flowers bloom in spring.

If I were making a movie of my story, I would have Rosalind Russell play our teacher Mrs. Lyle, because she was warm and gentle, but lanky and funny. She wore her dark hair back in a bun, and you knew she loved every one of us.

On the second day Mrs. Lyle asked, "Who knows the way to the office and can take the lunch money?"

I shyly raised my hand. Mrs. Lyle chose me.

I was thrilled and scared as I retraced my way back up the wide steps to the first floor, loving the heavy feel of the coins in the small square box. I remembered to turn at the water fountain across from the nurse's clinic, then past the school library to the office. I put the box up on the high counter and waited while Mrs. Webster, the school secretary, counted out the dimes and nickels. Then I returned with the box of heavy metal lunch tokens, handing it to Mrs. Lyle.

When she smiled I knew I had accomplished a noble task.

Mrs. Lyle became an extension of Mother. I looked to her for smiles of approval and attention. Later the whole world would become *the great mother* I would turn to for what I needed most —to know my accomplishments had earned me love.

Near Christmas, Mrs. Lyle said we were going to make a present for our parents. I was glowing inside since I had never given my mother a present before.

As Mrs. Lyle pressed my little hand in a round patty of clay for my handprint, I said, "This is for my Mother."

"Oh, now let's don't tell her," she said. "It will be a surprise."

Finally all the little handprints dried and were wrapped in white tissue paper with our names attached. Soon I was on my way home, carefully holding my handprint, dreaming of surprising Mother and making her smile, when all of a sudden I dropped it on the sidewalk. As I picked it up, I could already tell it was broken inside the tissue paper. My heart was broken in two, as sure as that handprint, and I had four more blocks to go.

Later, I gave it to Mother and cried again.

Mother said, "It's okay, Shug, it's okay."

I know it is NOT okay. It's broken.

Even when she stuck it back with airplane glue, it was a horrible reminder of how quickly things can go wrong, and how you can never *ever* fix things back right, even with airplane glue.

~

What I remember especially in first grade was that Miss Mattox, who was young and pretty, announced that she had invited our parents to visit our class. She said I was to take the wooden pointer and show where Casablanca was on the pull-down map of the world. My cue was, "Charlotte, can you show us where President Roosevelt met with the Allied leaders?"

On the day of our program, the class was so squirmy and tittery, like chicadees, as each parent arrived and made their way to one of the wooden folding chairs set up in back of the classroom. I was surprised that Grandma came though I would rather have had Mother there. I pointed to Casablanca, right on cue. The parents clapped, and I felt important that day. I'd been chosen to perform something special.

THE PIANO

The summer after first grade Mother paid $14 to have an ornate ebony upright piano moved to our house. I hung over the banisters watching the men heave the heavy piano up the four front steps and onto the porch. Grandma was holding the screen door open, wearing her long apron.

"They's not room for it," said Grandma in her Southern vernacular, and gave the man a *you'll-see* look.

Mother looked flustered, afraid she'd made a mistake, watching as they shoved it through the front door and slid it into the only space available, right in front of the little stained glass window with a broken cobalt-blue pane.

As soon as they'd gone, Mother sat right down and played the only song she ever knew, "Clayton's Grand March." She played with such zest and a remarkable command of the song. When she finished, she wheeled around on the piano stool and smiled at me so happy and proud, as if she'd just finished a concert at Carnegie Hall.

From that day on I wanted to sit down at the piano, play something grand, and turn around and smile. She played that song hundreds of times. Mother owned those thirty-two bars of "Clayton's Grand March."

Soon Mother found a young girl, Elizabeth Webster, to give me piano lessons, half a block down the street. Once a week Mother left Grandma fifty cents to give me. I put those two heavy quarters in the pocket of my favorite yellow cotton overalls. Under my arm I tucked a red John Thompson music book, and soon learned that it was the E-key on our piano that was missing its ivory cover.

(1943. First grade. My favorite yellow overalls.)

If I ever made a movie story of myself, I would have the character of *Shug* dress like I am in that photo, a character somewhere between Tom Sawyer and Scout in *To Kill A Mockingbird*.

Elizabeth gave me her used book of famous composers and had me learn one composer a week. She'd erased out her own answers. I loved knowing Elizabeth had written there before me.

"Bach, the Father of Music" was my first lesson. I was slow and needed many reminders, but Elizabeth was patient and kind.

One day after a lesson Elizabeth showed me her new little coupe parked by the curb. At the end of summer Mother said that Elizabeth had moved and I wouldn't have any more lessons.

I never saw Elizabeth again. She was gone, like James Alden, the boy that died. I missed her so much and kept that book about the composers for a long time.

Life was a lot about being separated from the people I became attached to. I hated leaving Miss Mattox, too, the sweetest teacher ever.

V IS FOR VICTORY

The best thing about second grade was World War II. The main reason being that gray-haired Miss Ruby Price was the crankiest teacher I ever had. I remember that day she yanked us into place, two by two, marching us down the wide marbled hallway for an important announcement about the war effort.

We sat squirming in long rows of wooden folding chairs, facing the maroon velour banner trimmed in gold fringe with a monogrammed J.C.H. Our school was named for Georgia's famous author, Joel Chandler Harris, whose Atlanta home, the Wren's Nest, was about a mile away.

At the front of the noisy room, our principal Miss Kendrick played a C-chord on the upright piano to bring us to attention. She was a short lady with gray braids pinned like ropes across the top of her head. She always had to play the chord twice for us to hush.

"Boys and girls," said Miss Kendrick, "raise your hand if someone in your family is serving in the war."

Hands went up everywhere. Already I felt so left out. I wanted to be able to raise my hand.

"Put your hands down," she said. "Now, *stand up* if your father is in the war."

A good number of boys and girls stood up, and Miss Kendrick asked a few where their fathers were stationed.

I didn't even have a father—well, not one I knew—much less one in the war. This was the first time I was publicly reminded of not having a father. I made a note to ask Grandma if she didn't know of someone I could claim, like little Bobby Sanders, who'd shouted out in baby-talk, 'Bernon, Bernon' because his big brother, Vernon, had just joined the Seabees.

"Boys and girls," continued Miss Kendrick, "I know how much you would like to help in the war effort. And you can. Today we're starting our victory badge campaign. Begin saving newspapers, tinfoil, and grease, so you can earn yours."

She held up a big round red, white, and blue pin-on button.

"Oh-o-oh!" A spontaneous murmur echoed off the high-ceilinged walls.

"After you earn your victory badge, you're a private. With additional collections you can earn a sergeant's ribbon, then a lieutenant's ribbon, all the way to general."

She held up a beautiful array of colorful satin ribbons. We clapped and there were shouts of *Whoopee!* and *Yippee!* Some of the bigger boys jumped up and saluted each other.

"Just call me general, sir!" said one.

Within me there was a stir of great excitement. Ah! Yes, here was a way for me to be a part of the war, at seven.

Thinking about those tasks was one thing—and *doing* all that collecting by myself was another. But Mrs. Gully and Mrs. Cornwell, who lived next door saved their tin cans for me. I put them in an orange mesh sack and when it was full, I sat on the back door-step and dumped the cans onto a wide, flat stepping stone. I used the big hammer to smash them flat.

On other days I rummaged along curbs for empty *Lucky Strike* packs and chewing gum wrappers. I carefully stripped off the tinfoil and mashed it into a small silver ball. Mother helped, too, by saving our empty soft metal *Ipana* toothpaste tubes, and I didn't have to be reminded to brush my teeth.

I was shy about taking my wagon up the sidewalk and asking neighbors for newspapers, but I managed to say, 'thank you,' and load a stack into my little red wagon. I pulled it back to Grandma's house, taking a stack at a time up our four front steps and around to the side porch, watching the stack get higher.

Finally I earned my victory badge. Miss Kendrick pinned it on me—a red, white, and blue badge with V-dot-dot-dash on it.

V is for Victory. Morse Code!

A secret code! I felt like I really belonged to the war and wore my badge to school every day.

Our campaign continued, and in the spring Miss Price announced, "Class, next month soldiers from Fort McPherson will be coming to our school. All children who have at least a lieutenant's rank will get to ride in a jeep."

A jeep ride! Now I had to figure out how to earn another ribbon. Grandma kept an empty Crisco can on the back of the stove for grease.

One day she announced the can was full.

"And don't be a'spilling it," she said, handing over the slippery can which had no lid.

I measured my steps with trepidation up to the corner, past the drugstore and the Georgia Milk—an ice cream parlor, that sold milkshakes and triple-decker ice cream cones—then to Smith's Grocery next door. Gingerly, I eased open Mr. Smith's tight screen door with its red, yellow, and blue Colonial Bread sign. I nudged my backside in, holding it open, then slowly let it close. I carefully walked down among the narrow rows of canned foods back to the meat counter. The meat man came out from behind the glass counter and took my precious can of grease.

While he weighed it, I stared at a new war poster on the wall behind him showing a giant drop of grease turning into a huge gold bullet. *How can grease turn into a bullet?* I wondered.

The meat man wiped his hands across his bloodstained apron and handed me a greasy slip of paper and a red meat token, which Grandma would later use for lamb chops, goose liver, stew-beef, bacon, or ground-round.

"I'm gettin' a lieutenant's ribbon with this!" I grinned, waving the slip of paper.

Oh, what a happy morning when Miss Price marched us outside for our reward. Six jeeps from Fort McPherson were lined up in the middle of the dusty red playground. *What a sight!*

I poked Sue Brown in front of me. "Look at that, wouldja, real jeeps!"

When my turn came, a young soldier with freckles and a wide grin said, "Up you go!"

Two soldiers, one on either side, swooped me up and swung me in like a sack of potatoes, dropping me on the back seat, squeezing in as many kids as they could. The jeep took off with a lurch, then bounced off the curb, tossing us around like Mexican jumping beans, our little heads bobbing up and down as the wind blew wildly through the girls' hair.

Boy! I thought, *When you're in the army, you can just drive anywhere you want to!*

We waved to anyone on White Street who had come out into their yard to see our merry convoy. I felt just like someone in those war newsreels I'd seen. All too soon our jeep bounced us back up over the curb and right back into the middle of the schoolyard.

"Down you go, little girl."

The same two soldiers lifted me down, and I felt like one of the G.I.s returning from the front lines. I saluted the freckled-faced one. He saluted me back.

In my school photo, dated May 9, 1944, I am proudly grinning with my victory badge pinned on a homemade dress trimmed with rickrack.

~

RATION BOOKS AND BLACKOUTS

Every morning Grandma slurped Eight O'Clock coffee from a thick white saucer at the wooden side table in the kitchen. She wore thick glasses with round silver rims and had false teeth.

By the time I got up for breakfast, her long muslin apron was already tied round her frail waist over a homemade cotton dress. Underneath she wore thick hose knotted at the knee.

She dunked half a Dutch Oven cake donut in the coffee and sucked on the juice. In sturdy black oxfords she moved to the tiny Magic Chef stove, stirring oatmeal in a double boiler on the back burner. She spooned it out for me, adding brown sugar, butter and canned milk, while the Germans were invading Europe.

By the summer of 1944, people were saying, *Ya' gotta have flat-feet or be cross-eyed to get out of goin' in the army.* Grandma's big ears were glued to the radio listening to H.V. Kaltenborn's nightly radio broadcasts, when she wasn't reading *The Atlanta Journal,* or gabbing on the phone.

We kept our phone out in the hall so the tenants could use it. It was one of those tall black kind with the receiver dangling from a cord and sat on a small three-legged half circle of a table next to the old family trunk.

"You remember Mattie?" said Grandma perched on the trunk talking to her sister. "Well, she has got herself a job working at the Bell Bomber Plant. Oh, you should see her goin' by. She's wearing pants, Alice, PANTS!"

All that summer I sat on the front steps and watched for anyone walking up the sidewalk to catch the streetcar, hoping I might learn something, especially waiting for Miss Mattie Shelton to pass by wearing her gray shirt and pants and bandana. She would swing her lunchbox like she was going to do something important. Sometimes she said 'hello,' and I kept hoping she would stop and tell me how you make a B-29.

During that time Grandma told me we'd been issued ration books, and I remember she showed me hers—a booklet the size of a postcard with little gray and green stamps to be torn out.

"No stamp, no sugar," said Grandma.

I was standing on the rim of her rocker that day, looking at a big blackhead right in the middle of Grandma's ear, and noticing her gray hair loosely gathered up into a knot on her head, skewered with long hairpins.

"Look'a here," she said pointing with her thick, curved fingernail. "They's only two stamps for shoes. That's all we get for a whole durn year, me'n, you'n, Totsy. Two pairs each!"

Once when I wanted canned pears, Grandma said, "All the country's money's going to feed them soldiers, makin' uniforms, boots, helmets, guns, tanks and 'bums.'" She pronounced bombs, 'bums.' She said I couldn't have canned pears, "They got sugar. They're rationed, so stop whining!"

She carried on and on. "Listen, if you use up all your coffee stamps, you can't git no more, even if you have the money, unless you're Mr. Charlie Ray."

Grandma was purely driven to have her cup of Eight O'Clock coffee every morning.

"You can use the coffee stamp in my book," I said.

She lifted her eyebrows, peering over at me from under her silver-rimmed glasses, "I kno-o-w."

Then she said she bet Mr. Charlie Ray would never have to go without *his* coffee, because he was in the black-market and that was probably how come he'd lost his left arm—that or bootlegging.

Mr. Charlie Ray, his wife Estelle, and little Charlie Jr. lived up the street in a nice new brick house with an extra lot beside it. He drove a shiny black Ford with the window rolled down, propping his stump on the edge. His pinned-up sleeve would be flapping in the wind as he flew down Holderness Street.

I pictured Mr. Charlie Ray getting his arm smashed off because he'd left it hanging out the window sometime or other when a black market truck sideswiped him as he was outrunning the cops.

What I wished was that Mr. Charlie Ray would get me some black-market bubblegum. When Setzer's Drug Store got in a fresh box of two hundred pieces, I would run to Grandma, begging for a nickel for five pieces, which was all you were allowed.

As soon as I was back out the drugstore door, I would stop on the sidewalk and could already feel my mouth bursting to chew as I unwrapped a piece. I even licked off the sugary powder coating from the wax paper comics that came inside.

I remember practicing blowing bubbles because I always had dreams of being the champion of something. I chewed each piece of Fleer's Dubble Bubble for as long as I could, then at night I stuck the pink wad under a curve on the knob of the bedpost. In the morning sometimes there would be a piece of brown paint stuck to the bottom. I wondered if it would kill me, but I stuck it back in my mouth anyway, *without telling*.

One evening Mother brought home a whole box of Hershey bars that were given out to the girls in her office. Grandma said they were probably black-market and vowed she wouldn't eat any. Mother put the box in the bottom drawer of Grandma's chifforobe.

"Shug, you can have only two squares at a time," said Mother breaking off the first two that had an H printed on them.

Um-mmm. I let each chocolatey square melt on my tongue, making it last as long as I could.

I loved Hershey bars.

~

Grandma was on the phone again. The word was out that the United States might even be bombed. A German sub had been spotted off Jacksonville Beach, Florida. Citizens were told to get blackout curtains, or shades, or put up blankets on all the windows. Each neighborhood was organized and assigned an air raid warden.

"Well, did'ja hear the news, Alice?" said Grandma perched on the edge of the big trunk again. "Now they're a'tellin' us to have a bucket of wet sand ready in case one of them incendiary 'bums' falls through our roof. Don't that beat all?"

I remember one night during a blackout, we were sitting huddled around together in Grandma's bedroom listening to the radio. The coal was popping in the warm stove. Grandma was in her big black rocker. Mother had pulled up Grandma's vanity bench, and I was in my little rocker—like the three bears.

If I were making a movie, I'd have Agnes Moorehead as Grandma and demure Teresa Wright as Mother.

Suddenly we heard a man's heavy footsteps on the side porch next to the bedroom. I shuddered, thinking it might be a real Nazi, like the one that wound up in Greer Garson's back yard in *Mrs. Miniver*. There was a knock on the door and a man's voice said, "Miz Chap, this is Mr. Sewell. I can see light comin' from this side door window here. Dowse that light or make that shade to fit closer."

Grandma opened the door. "You scared us to death."

I peeked around her and saw Mr. Sewell in his white air raid warden's helmet. He was a nice friendly man I liked.

"Close your door, Miz Chap," he said, "You're lettin' out even more light."

~

I thought I might like having Mr. Sewell for a father. I remember that once Mr. Sewell got up some boxing matches in his backyard for his son Horace and the neighborhood boys. He roped off a square space and laid out some planks for seats. We kids had to pay a nickel to come watch. I think he wanted his son to be a prize fighter. Grandma said Horace was a weaklin'.

I knew all about Joe Louis from the newsreels. I thought if I were Mr. Sewell's son, I'd put on those boxing gloves and give everybody a good match.

The war set me to thinking about so many things, especially about men who could go off and fight, and do a lot of other worthy things, and here we were all huddled around a coal stove, no use at all.

~

Chapter 4

My Father's Hobby Was the Dictionary

I NEVER KNEW MY FATHER and didn't pay much attention to his absence until I was around seven, in 1943, when so many men had gone off to war. Then I was wishing that I had a father, or *someone* I could claim that was fighting for America.

I remember I was sitting on the toilet dangling my chubby legs while Mother was taking a bath, soaping her arms with a thin washrag.

"Tell me about my father," I said.

"I've already told you."

She held out the soapy washrag. "Wash Mother's back."

I squished soapy water up and down her back, noticing the freckles on her shoulders.

"Tell me again," I pleaded.

"He sold insurance."

"What else?"

"He was the treasurer of St. Luke's."

"And. . .?"

I already knew what was coming.

"And, he read the dictionary," said Mother.

"Was he tall or short?"

"Short, I told you. That's all I know," she said.

She wasn't going to tell me any more this time, either, so I let the washrag slide back into the soapy water and scooted to the back-porch bedroom, popped my fingers in my mouth and burrowed myself in the musty old quilt.

I just wanted to know a little more about my father.

~

Mother was twenty-seven when I was born. My father was forty-four. I found that out from rummaging in the old black trunk and finding my birth certificate. There was my tiny inked footprint from the Crawford Long Hospital in Atlanta with all our names together. It was like I existed with a real family that one day.

I never even saw a photo of my father. When his monthly $34 check came in the mail, sometimes I'd just hold it, noticing his scrawly handwriting in the corner:

C. W. Ashurst
#777 St. Charles Ave.

When I was a little older, I asked Mother how they met.

"Well, we started meeting at the drugstore in the building downstairs. He kept saying we'd be good together. Mama didn't like him though . . . said he was nearer to *her* age, but I married him anyway."

Here's what else I'd gleaned: Mother and my father had lived in the rented part of Grandma's house when they first married. Then I came along in 1936. Not long after that, they moved to a little apartment in Decatur, Georgia—probably because I was crying and Grandma had kicked them out. I say that because I'd heard Grandma saying to prospective tenants, "No babies, y'hear? No babies!"

My father was divorced and already had two daughters, Betty and Sarah, eight and ten. Mother said sometimes the girls came to visit and she would let them push my baby carriage around the square in Decatur. She said everyone commented, "Oh, that's the prettiest baby."

You know how that is, though, everyone says that about every baby. Still it was nice to hear that about me, especially about a time I knew nothing about—a time when I had both a mother and a father—and even two half-sisters.

Here's my little scenario: It was a rainy day when my father stopped off in Jacob's Drugstore in the William-Oliver Building where they both worked right in the heart of Atlanta. I think he noticed how young and pretty Mother was—pretty as Clara Bow, the "it" girl of his day. Mother would've been flattered that an older man paid her all that cheap, easy, soda fountain attention, as he reminded her of her own papa.

Mother always referred to my father as "Ashurst," maybe hearing that from a salesman hailing my father at the soda fountain.

'Say, Ashurst, who's this pretty little miss?'

Men spoke like that back then—some vestige of British formality and a 30s sophistication—I'd seen that in the movies.

I think they probably got to know each other drinking fountain Cokes, never even having a real date before he popped the question. Mother said for their honeymoon they went to Toccoa Falls in North Georgia.

Here's what else I think: I think my father was one kind of person in that drugstore and another person once they married. I pictured him in a second-hand chair with blue floral slipcovers, a floor lamp with a yellowed shade and fluttery tassels. He'd have his head buried like a gopher in a hole, reading the dictionary and hating to hear me cry.

I asked Mother how come she divorced him.

"He wouldn't give me any money to buy dresses," she said.

That's all she ever said.

Then I pictured Mother standing solemnly in front of three dresses hanging limply from three pegs on the back of a door. But in my child's mind, not having enough dresses didn't seem like enough of a reason to divorce.

Another time Mother said that sometimes the neighbors across the hall would invite my father in for a highball and he'd go, and she did not like that one bit. Then she let it slip that my father once held a butcher knife over my baby bed. So I guess there was a *lot more* going on that I will never know.

~

I nearly met my father once. Really! It still excites me to remember it. And this was for real— better than anything I could come up with for a movie story.

One Saturday Mother and I rode the bus downtown and stopped off in her office building. As Mother was signing in on the weekend elevator check-in sheet, I noticed above her signature a scrawly "C.W. Ashurst," exactly the way I'd seen it written on those monthly checks.

I couldn't believe it. *"Oh, no!"* My head jerked around, *"Where? Where?"* as if I might spot him, because he had signed out just five minutes earlier. I was excited and scared, too, as the elevator doors slowly closed and we began ascending to the fifth floor where she worked.

"Mother, what would you have done if we'd met him on the elevator?"

"I would've said, 'This is your daughter.'"

And she dismissed it—just like that—in her matter-of-fact way. Oh, but I went around with that elevator dream in my head for years. I kept thinking that maybe I'd bump into him again and see him in person. He'd be wearing a hat. All men did then. He'd tip it at me, smile and reach out his hand . . .

~

Once when I went to Mother's office by myself, I was in the elevator alone, and instead of pressing the elevator button for the fifth floor where Mother worked, I got up enough nerve to press the button for the fourteenth floor where *he* worked.

I stepped out into the small empty landing, alone, looking at the heavy lettered doors to the John Hancock offices, which had pebbly glass windows you couldn't see through. I was afraid to go in, and felt ashamed for even thinking about doing so, as if I might be trespassing in stuff that was none of my business. I just stood there with no gumption, whatsoever, to open the door and go in.

One year I got a *Webster's Dictionary* for Christmas. I sat on the bed under a little red gooseneck lamp I'd hung precariously on the beaverboard wall. I opened to the first page and wondered if my father started with the A's and read straight through, or if he memorized all the definitions?

~

When I was sixteen and had occasion to be riding the trolley across town, down Ponce de Leon Avenue, I'd hold my breath watching for Highland Avenue. One block down was St. Charles Avenue— I'd looked it up on a map. If the trolley came to a stop, I'd look as far down that street as I could. Many times I thought about hopping right off.

I imagined that I'd knock on his door, #777. It would be a dark brown wood without a door knocker. I'd have to knock again. He'd crack the door open a tiny bit, because he was shy, wearing a ratty dark plaid bathrobe, and I'd say, 'Hi, I'm your daughter.'

I must've played that scene about a million times in my head. But I couldn't imagine past that. I figured our meeting would be too awkward and probably embarrass him and me both.

I tried not to think about him too much, though, because too much of that empty feeling— well, it slows you down in life. Sometimes it's better not to know. If he'd really wanted to see me, he could've. I figured I was doing us both a favor.

Other times though, I'd be riding the trolley and find myself looking around, wondering if one of those strangers, right across the aisle, might not be my father.

I imagined if only we could meet accidentally, somehow things might work just for that one moment. We could meet, then rush off with only that single memory of what we looked like to each other. Like on that elevator.

~

Maybe it would've been different if I'd been a boy, then I would've known straight away what to do with my life. Maybe my father would've come and visited me, and taken me to a ball game, or maybe I would've had the nerve to visit his office and introduce myself and tell him I was his son. I'd say, 'Mother said you read the dictionary,' and see what he'd say to that.

But that's hindsight, isn't it? A twice-told tale. I'm just starting in to tell my story and already I'm making myself sad to even think that way. You can't change the past.

~

My father died at age seventy-five. Mother sent me a copy of his obituary from *The Atlanta Journal*. His other two daughters Betty and Sarah were the only two survivors listed.

I wondered if maybe Mother could've just *told* me about it, so I wouldn't have had to see my name NOT listed, but then Mother was so matter-of-fact; she was a little like Grandma in that way, not thinking about my feelings.

And maybe she sent it to remind me that she had been right, all along, to keep us apart. Even though I was thirty years old, I got sad and lonely again, reading over that obituary.

Who am I, anyway? I asked.

~

Some years after that, I was studying to take the G.R.E. and reading a paperback entitled *Six Weeks to Words of Power* by Wilfred Funk. At the beginning of each section is a quote, such as:

Each word at first was a stroke of genius. — Emerson
Words are the voice of the heart. — Confucius

On page 39 was the quote:

Most men paint, fish or collect stamps.
My hobby is the dictionary. — Ashurst

When I saw that quote, I was flabbergasted. I wanted to rush out and grab someone and say, 'Look, look, THIS IS MY FATHER! I know it!'

What a story that must've been if he really loved the dictionary that much, and someone like Mr. Funk heard about it.

But I just saved the paperback after I finished taking the G.R.E. and put it back up on the shelf. Even now, I occasionally take it down and turn to page 39 and read the quote—just to be sure it's still there. Or sometimes when I'm in a bookstore, I'll look to see if my father's quote is there, right in with the quotes of Confucius and Emerson. And sure 'nuf, the last time I looked, it was still there.

Most men paint, fish or collect stamps.
My hobby is the dictionary. — Ashurst.

~

Chapter 5

Riding the Streetcar with Evelyn Keyes

MOTHER HAD A FAVORITE STREETCAR STORY. When she started it, her voice would take on a hushed tone.

"Did I evah tell you the story about ridin' the streetcar with Evelyn Keyes?" she would say, her green eyes narrowing, as she eased into this story like it was something sacred.

"Well, I was going to my job downtown, and just two stops from where I got on, Evelyn Keyes would get on at Lawton Street because she lived down on Sells Avenue. I'd save her a seat and motion to her so she could sit by me. Evelyn told me she was a tap dancer, and that she was going to be an actress one day, so I wanted to get to know her better. Then Evelyn didn't show up anymore, and I didn't see her again. The next thing I knew, she was in *Gone with the Wind*."

Well, that was Mother's entire little story!

Every time she'd tell it I'd keep hoping there'd be a different ending, like maybe Evelyn Keyes would remember Mother befriending her on the streetcar and invite Mother to the gala premier in Atlanta, and Mother would get to sit right next to Clark Gable, and then I'd have a story to tell at school.

I thought Mother secretly wished she'd gone to Hollywood and become a star, and I wished that for Mother, too, because then I'd be living there and not sleeping on some lumpy sagging Beautyrest mattress on an enclosed backporch.

~

The earliest I remember riding the streetcar was when Mother and I would make the long Sunday trip to visit her sister, Gladys. We walked a block to the streetcar stop, then transferred to the bus marked Oglethorpe. I'd be all tired out by the time the bus stopped at Roxboro Road located in Buckhead, a nice section of Atlanta with no sidewalks. We still had to walk two more long blocks.

Red-faced Uncle Marvin would meet us at the door, jiggling a glass with ice. "Well, look at little Sha-Sha," he'd say, and that made me feel special. He would usually hold up his glass toward Mother, "Totsy, how about a highball after that long trip?"

Mother always said, "No thank you, Marvin."

~

Now Aunt Gladys wasn't a bit prettier than Mother, but she dressed and acted smarter and had more get-up-and-go. She had snagged Uncle Marvin, a Western Union lawyer, who had grown up in a big house on Ashby Street, and belonged to the West End Golf Club.

Cousin Sonny, who was four years older than I, would head straight for Mother, tugging at her hand, wanting her attention. He was their only child, and Mother was crazy about Sonny since she spent a lot of time with him before I was born.

I didn't like Sonny one bit and didn't want to share my mother with anyone, especially a big fat nine-year-old who loved to knock my croquet ball as far away as possible.

She had trained him to call her "Aunt Margaret," not "Totsy," and she was always reminding everyone that she had bought him his first suit at three—a size ten.

I learned later that Aunt Gladys had briefly taken in Mother and me after Mother's break-up. So I see now I had invaded little Sonny's four-year-old space with his mother and his doting Aunt Margaret. No wonder he had no use for me.

(Aug. 1937. Me, Mother, Aunt Gladys, Sonny, and Spot, the dog.)

I remember how much I loved their white brick bungalow with a stone porch and curved steps. The living room was a French rustic style with exposed beams, a white mantle, and a big bay window—all of which seemed like a Hollywood home to me.

I delighted in stepping down into the small dining room where long lace curtains were blowing in the breeze. There was a lace cloth on the dining room table, and a buffet with a shiny silver tea service. A single French-paned door led to the small graveled patio with an umbrella and white Adirondack chairs.

I loved the small kitchen with a big walk-in pantry. I especially loved the colorful wooden sign on the wall with names of items like cheese, milk, fruit, bread, and potatoes. It had red wooden pegs lined up along the bottom. I thought about how much I wanted to be the one to put a red peg by *milk* or *cheese*. Then Sonny would come and interrupt, tugging at Mother's arm.

"Aunt Mahg-vet, come look! Father made us a badminton court."

Uncle Marvin was getting out the racquets. "C'mon, Totsy, let's have a game."

We would trek down their steep back steps and through the narrow yard enclosed with high hedges. This area was where Uncle Marvin put up the wickets when we played croquet near the persimmon tree.

Behind their white garage, Uncle Marvin had leveled off the ground and marked out an area with white lines and a net.

"Well, look at this! My goodness, like a real court," Mother said in her delightful way.

I watched as Mother skipped to hit the shuttlecock, swinging her racquet through the summer breeze. She laughed, especially when she missed, having such a good time, forgetting about the long trip back and another week of stamping out charge-a-cards for Rich's customers.

Mother seemed so happy on those visits. Maybe because her older sister was watching out for me and she could be free of being a parent all by herself. Maybe it was hard on Mother to have responsibility for me and live crammed in on the back porch of the house she grew up in as a child and have to hear Grandma's daily rancor.

On the way home on the streetcar, I would lean on Mother's soft arm, listening to her wistful sighs. Maybe she was wishing she could have a pretty house and thinking that Gladys was smarter than she was and had made something of herself.

But I could be all wrong about that, too.

~

When Mother worked late, especially in winter, I remember waiting in my maple rocker by the coal stove in Grandma's bedroom, sucking my two middle fingers and twisting my hair. A yellow glow from the dull lampshade cast shadows on the faded rose-print wallpaper.

My rocking chair had a worn out music box that once plinked a tune. I was almost too big for that chair, but I didn't want to give it up. The only sound now was the thin wire hitting the bare floor—*plink-plink, plink-plink.*

Grandma was in her black rocker, leaning in occasionally to open up the stove door, stir the coal with the iron poker, then pick up the heavy tongs to clamp a lump of black coal from the tin scuttle and shove it in the flaming mouth. Little sparks of embers would shoot up—pop! crunch!—as the smaller coals settled. She slammed the heavy stove door, then leaned back with a certain amount of satisfaction, listening to H.V. Kaltenborn's broadcast news, lifting her heels just enough to keep herself rocking.

"*Um*-um-um-*um*?" I asked plaintively, without removing my fingers from my mouth, which meant, '*When's Mother coming home?*'

"I told you, she's a' workin' late," answered Grandma.

Since my rocker sat near the side-porch door with a window, I could hear any footsteps that came down the sidewalk. At the faintest approach of each new set of steps, I listened to see if they belonged to Mother.

I knew just how she walked.

Rock, rock, suck fingers, twist hair, rock, rock, listen . . . then I heard them. Mother's footsteps! My heart beat faster. My fingers popped out of my mouth.

"It's Mother!"

I sat up straight and cocked my head, hearing the *click-click, click-click* of Mother's high heels turning into our walkway, climbing up the four steps to the front porch, and walking around to the side-porch door.

I waited like a happy puppy. Mother might have a surprise, like an old eraser that fit on the end of an office pencil, or a used stamp pad and date-stamper with numbers I could change and make it 1923 or 1965.

A SILENT MOVIE STREETCAR STORY

One Sunday on the way home from a movie at the Loew's Grand, we stopped by a fruit stand and bought some big purple Concord grapes. We had invited Kay, an only child, to go with us. On the streetcar the three of us took a side seat, with Kay and me on either side of Mother, who soon began fishing grapes out of the little brown sack.

"Don't swallow the seeds," Mother cautioned us. "Put 'em back in here," she said, folding the top down all around, so there was a nice opening. As she was fishing out the next round of grapes, one fell onto the aisle of the streetcar into one of the narrow wooden ridges that kept water from collecting. As the streetcar rattled along the tracks, we began watching the grape roll up and down the ridge. A passenger got on and just barely missed stepping on the grape. That made Mother titter.

We kept on watching the grape rolling a little, then stopping. Then Mother began to anticipate the fate of the grape with each new passenger. As she spied someone waiting at the next stop, she clutched her purse and braced herself, like someone in a silent movie. We were eagerly caught up in Mother's emotion.

"Look, Shug, here comes one!"

The streetcar stopped for the passenger. I grabbed the edge of my seat, holding my breath. We watched as a matronly woman climbed aboard and dropped in her car token. Mother clutched my arm and held her breath as if we had some kind of ownership in the life of this poor grape. She made an excited sound, sucking in air through her clenched teeth.

"Sss-sss-sss!"

The woman's sturdy oxford missed the grape. Passengers around us quietly began enjoying our game. The tension mounted as we approached the next car stop. Any second now, someone's foot would smash the grape to smithereens! Mother kept one eye on the position of the grape and one eye on the foot of a new passenger, just boarding. Then all of us were riveted on the sole of a huge uplifted brown brogan turning to come down the aisle. Mother's fingers squeezed my arm and, again, Mother sucked in another breath.

"Sss-sss-sss! Shug!"

The passenger's shoe barely missed the grape.

Tears streamed from behind Mother's rimless glasses. She hugged herself to contain her hysterics. I laughed, too, and looked at Kay, who was thoroughly enjoying Mother's antics.

When the streetcar went around a curve, the grape disappeared down the aisle, never to be seen again.

~

As I got older, Grandma would let me go all the way to the corner to meet Mother when she came home from work. I'd hang out in front of Stanfield's grocery, swinging around on the big greasy black pole outside the store, and peer down those long streetcar tracks on Lucille Avenue, waiting for Mother to step off the streetcar so we could walk home together.

~

When I reflect on the inevitable nature of growing from an adoring child to a sulky teenager to eventually leaving home, I'm glad Mother still had her little Evelyn Keyes story tucked away, like a precious jewel in her grab bag of entertaining things to say and do, and that she could tell it again, in that hushed tone.

"Did I evah tell you the story about riding the streetcar with Evelyn Keyes?"

~

Chapter 6

By Hook or By Crook

GRANDMA LOVED EIGHT O'CLOCK COFFEE, radio soap operas, and *The Atlanta Journal*. A widow in her fifties, she never really recovered from the car wreck in 1929, nor from her husband's tragic death. She never spoke of either. All her family were buried back at the Mt. Paran Baptist Church cemetery. Sometimes she hummed a little of "Rock of Ages."

Once I remember us being in the cold living room with only the light of a gray day coming through the thin lacy curtains of the window by the side porch. Grandma opened up a worn black Baptist hymnal to "Abide with Me" and played a couple of measures. I heard her tough yellow nails clacking on the keys. I didn't know Grandma could even play the piano, or that she knew how to read the music.

There was so much I didn't know about her.

As far as I could tell Grandma took a hit-or-miss approach to life. If anything broke, she waited until the insurance man came to collect the monthly premium, then she'd hand him his quarter and say, "Mr. Honea, wouldja take a look at this here electric cord? It's shootin' out sparks ever' time we plug it in." If the policy man didn't fix it, it didn't get fixed.

That's how she kept things running, *by hook or by crook*. It's amazing how little you can do and still survive. Buy white bread. Read *The Atlanta Journal*. Listen to WSB radio. Buy a new Easter hat.

~

Grandma said mean things to Mother though—that's what I didn't like about her. Mother was always telling me this story about Grandma taking *her* to school.

She'd start off with, "*You* know *Mama*, she didn't care if she hurt your feelings or *not*."

Then Mother would shift into a special dramatic reenactment and continue, "The day I started first grade, I begged her, I said, 'Mama, please, oh, PLEASE, PLEASE, Mama, don't tell the teacher my name is Totsy. Tell her my name is Margaret.' But when the teacher asked my name, Mama said, 'TOTSY CHAPPELEAR,' and I crawled up under the teacher's desk. That's how Mama was, you know, she didn't care if she hurt your feelings, or not."

Then Mother would laugh like it didn't matter, but the more I heard that story, the more I knew that Mother's feelings *were* hurt and that she'd played second fiddle to her older sister.

I couldn't stand anyone being mean to Mother.

~

I remember Grandma leaving me with the maid.

"Esther's coming. I'm a-goin' downtown," said Grandma lifting the lid off the butter beans, giving them a stir. She took off her apron, walking into her bedroom next to the kitchen. I followed and perched on her iron-framed bed to watch. She took out a long bony corset from a drawer in the tall chifforobe, then fitted it around her thin body, hooking together about a million little hooks and eyes.

Soon I heard the back screen door creak, and Esther's long loping walk resounded on the planks in the hall. Esther was none too friendly to me.

Grandma called, "Git a dozen rolls when the Dutch Oven man comes."

"Yes'm," said Esther, putting her bulging black purse high up on a kitchen shelf.

"And watch th' butter beans don't burn."

"Yes'm."

Grandma sat down at her vanity dresser with the fold-in mirrors to pin on a bunch of stiff violets near the 'V' of the wide lace-trimmed white collar of her crepy dress with a large flowered print. She dabbed on lavender toilet water, stuffed a wadded-up handkerchief in her purse, and donned a dark blue straw hat, trimmed with red cherries.

Sometimes when Grandma went next door to Mrs. Cornwell's, I'd stand in front of those vanity mirrors and put on that same navy blue hat, pulling the thin elastic band around the back of my hair, as I'd seen her do. I'd even sucked on one of those shiny, inviting-looking lacquered red cherries, but what a disappointment.

Grandma jammed more and more things into her big black pocketbook, moving faster and faster, anxious to catch the streetcar, telling Esther what else to do while she was gone.

After Grandma left, I watched Esther wash clothes in the bathtub using a scrub board, or watched her hang them in the yard. Sometimes I watched her iron. Sometimes I just stayed out on the porch coloring a page in a coloring book.

Esther would fix me a sandwich for lunch and call me in.

"Chile here's yo' lunch."

~

When the Sanders moved in the house two doors up the street, little Bobby was always coming over eating a raisin pie because his daddy drove a Merita Bread truck. Grandma would shoo Bobby with the broom, saying, "Git off this porch, you're a'droppin' crumbs and we'll get ants."

About that time a young couple moved in. Mr. Young had lost a leg in the war and stayed home. Sometimes when Bobby would be in the front yard, Mr. Young would call him to his narrow screen door and give him money to get him a pack of "Luckies."

One day, in the front yard Bobby said to me, "I seen it."

"Seen what?" I asked.

"Mr. Young's wonkus." he said pointing to the screen door.

Apparently Mr. Young went around naked except for his truss in the summer heat.

One day when Grandma had left me with a maid, we were sitting on the bed in the back bedroom when the heavy door to the hallway slowed opened, and there stood Mr. Young naked except for his truss.

"Shade yo' eyes, chile," said the maid. Then without looking up, she mumbled, "Go on, Mr. Young. Go on over t' y'side."

I remember the creepy feel of a naked body in a truss standing in the doorway of the room I slept in every night. I don't know if Grandma or Mother ever knew.

~

I have other early memories of waiting in the kitchen with throbbing earaches while Grandma warmed up sweet oil in a pan of water to drop into my ear with some cotton. I remember mustard plasters for the croup, doses of nasty liquids being poked at me in tablespoons too big for my mouth, and horrible bitter-tasting brown pills she crushed and put in a teaspoon.

When I got chicken-pox, Grandma swabbed my sores with Calamine lotion. I remember her putting a cold rag on my head for measles. I also remember Sal Hepatica, Castor Oil, Fletcher's Castoria, the chalky taste of Milk of Magnesia, and a lot of enemas. Yet in her slip-shod manner, Grandma managed to keep me from all major diseases, accidents and afflictions.

~

I was mostly handy for Grandma's indulences. She'd open her purse with the two gold orbs that snapped shut like her mouth when she'd had enough, saying, "Here, take this and run up to the store and git six slices of gooseliver and some of them chocolate marshmallow cookies."

Once Grandma baked me a birthday cake.

"Stay outta this kitchen," she said that day and shut the door, which was *always* left open. I tried peeping through the keyhole, but all I could see was the back of her long faded dress at the side table. I could hear her beating up the batter in a heavy bowl.

I had to wait all afternoon till Mother came home. After supper Grandma brought out a lopsided cake. The boiled white icing had cooked too long and the candles made big cracks in the top where she'd poked them in. But I did like her lemon-cheese filling.

The only present I ever remember being from Grandma was that year. It was a brownish colored piggy bank in the shape of a bust of General MacArthur with a slot in his Army hat for coins. Grandma looked at the bank and said, "MacArthur's the only general in the war with a lick a'sense!"

THE VICTORY GARDEN

During the war everyone was asked to plant a Victory Garden. Soon Grandma hired a black man who came up our back alley with a "war mule" to plow up a place in the middle of our backyard, right between the fish pond and the little rock patio.

Afterwards, she gave him a jar of ice water and a dime, then took off her apron and announced, "C'mon, we're going to the seed store."

She went to the chifforobe and got out her big black purse, and we set out for the seed store at the corner, next to Smith's grocery.

I'd only seen big burlap sacks sagging against the hot store front and never had occasion to go in. Oh, but that day I remember how dark and cool it felt inside. Heavy sacks of chicken feed were stacked up on the hard-packed dirt floor.

While Grandma looked at the packets of vegetable seeds, I peered into the low wooden seed bins, running my hand through the inviting pink, yellow, and brown kernels, finally plopping down on a big soft feed sack to wait. I noticed that each sack had a different printed design.

I remembered that Mrs. Cornwell, our neighbor, had made me a brown and orange plaid dress out of feed sack material with toy soldiers all over it.

(School photo age 8. 1944)

The next day I watched as Grandma took a bow rake and dragged big red clods of dirt to the edges as she leveled off the inside part to start her garden. Then she broke off some limbs and made little stobs to tie strings for rows.

"This here's how we done it back at the ol' homeplace," she said, leaning over and dropping in a bean seed.

"Here, you do some," she said, pouring out a few hard white seeds into my hand. As I dropped in a bean, she raked dirt over it. "Tha's right, keep a'goin.'" Then she took the seed packet and stuck it on the stob at the end of the row.

When Mother got home from work, she filled up the galvanized watering can at the outside water spigot and watered all the rows. She liked doing it. We all wanted to help with the war effort.

And one summer morning Grandma pointed with the hoe.

"Look'a there, a bean's a'comin'," she said. "They's another."

I stooped to take a look, and then to marvel for a moment at a tiny green bean growing from a white blossom.

And thus began the wonder and magic of gardening.

Soon after that, Grandma was out on the porch hailing Mr. Whatley walking up the street on the other side.

"Mr. Whatley," she yelled across the banisters, "I picked a mess of beans from my victory garden this morning."

And now I remember hearing "Coming In On a Wing and a Prayer," on the radio. I pictured a soldier kneeling on the wing of a plane in mid-air, and thinking that somehow we'd helped him.

THE VEGETABLE MAN

In summers I drove Grandma crazy because there were no children to play with except for little Lester, three years younger. All I heard was, "Stay on the front porch," or, "Don't go outta this back yard!"

It was just Grandma and me and nothing to do. I played jack stones on the porch. I had a can of fiddlesticks. I marked off hopscotch on the walkway with chalk.

As soon as I heard the jangling sound of metal scales banging the sides of the vegetable truck, I'd yell, "It's Mr. Smith, Grandma, let's get some fresh peaches."

I bolted off the concrete stoop beside the front steps, running ahead down the sidewalk. Mr. Smith had once given me a handful of goobers—raw peanuts—smelling like cool damp dirt.

When the sound of the vegetable truck was heard, neighbor ladies grabbed their coin purses, converging like crows in starched cotton dresses, as the dark green truck with wooden slats swayed down the street and parked in the next block.

Along the sides of the truck Mr. Smith had fashioned little bins to show off his fresh-picked garden delights, still smelling of earth and rain and sunshine. City ladies—first generation off the farm ladies—eagerly bought Elberta peaches, purple hull peas, fresh okra, fat red tomatoes, tender yellow crookneck squash, English peas, mouth-watering ears of corn, cantaloupe, and watermelon. Each woman could walk all the way around, inspecting and selecting.

Jolly Mr. Smith wore ironed blue denim overalls and a straw hat. I watched as he pulled a knife from his pocket and stripped off the hard outer part of a purple stalk of sugar cane and handed me a thin sliver.

"Taste this, little girl," he said with a twinkle.

Lord, it was sweet!

"How much them pole beans?" someone asked.

"Lord, I usta pick beans and chop cotton, *both*," said another.

"Me 'n you!" was a reply.

"Got some real nice butter beans, ladies," said Mr. Smith, snapping open a fat green hull, revealing four plump speckled butter beans, every bit as tempting as the beans Jack got for the family cow.

"Speckled! Look at that, Grandma! Let's get some."

I darted past her to get a closer look at those magic beans cradled in Mr. Smith's rough palm. I thought I'd like to throw some out my window, climb up a magic beanstalk, outwit an ogre, and bring home some golden eggs, myself.

~

I didn't know those ladies, had never been in their houses, but I sensed they were happy that morning because they were smiling and gabby. Mostly those ladies on the other side of the street stayed shut up in their houses, or sat on porches with just the tops of their heads showing on enclosed balustrades. If one of them called me by my name, it always surprised me.

I knew these ladies might be buying okra to fry up for supper for a husband who once thought it was a bright idea to move to the city as had my grandparents. For the most part, they still *talked country* and their grown children had all moved away. And now, it was just the two of them left to share tonight's peach cobbler and talk about how glad they were that the war was over.

I couldn't imagine what *chopping cotton* might be, but I could tell from the tone of their voices that it was "mighty" hard, as was much of life on a rural Georgia farm. Yet they all seemed to have had a similar affection for those farmlands, mentioning plows, mules, a hog-killin', and cool well water.

Yes, I think those ladies were happy around the vegetable truck, remembering their childhood. And Grandma, too, though she *never* told me much of anything, other than saying they had eaten possum with sweet potatoes, and I think maybe she knew how to churn.

But I can tell you as a lonely offspring, as one who grew up in a neighborhood with mostly old people and no children, I came to be no more than an unintended consequence of that generation that moved off the farm for the big city life. I had no chores. There were no chickens to feed, or eggs for me to bring in, or a bucket of corn cobs to slop a hog. I was a pest, of no use at all except to run to the store once in a while for store-bought cookies, lamb chops, and DeVoe snuff for a maid, who came to wash our clothes in the tub with a scrub board.

~

Grandma handed Mrs. Smith a bunch of beets, a cantaloupe, fresh corn, and some pole beans to weigh. I noticed Mrs. Smith's beady eyes peering out from under the sheltering hood of her feed-sack bonnet, pressing her thin lips together, carefully weighing the long green pole beans. She kept her eye on the scales, and with nary a word she took the correct amount out of Grandma's outstretched palm. Then Mrs. Smith dropped the beans in a used brown sack and handed it to Grandma who turned looking for me.

"Git up off that curb and take this cantaloupe!"

I was sprawled out trying to fix the loose gauze and adhesive tape bandage dangling from my big toe. I'd stubbed it from running barefoot on the sidewalk.

"Git up, I said!" said Grandma.

"I don't need this ol' thing anyway," I said flinging it in the gutter. Dirt particles had stuck to the adhesive. A stumped toe was like a war wound since I could get a little sympathy and feel like a hero all at the same time. This one was red, raw, oozing yellowish fluid, with a piece of the toenail scraped away. It was the kind of stumped toe you could stop someone on the street to show off—not that there was ever anyone around—but still, I was always aware of ammunition for a little attention.

We walked back home together carrying our little mess of happiness between us. As soon as Grandma got home, she started washing and cutting up the beets to put on to boil.

"Go put peroxide on that toe."

I kept hanging around watching, waiting for something better to do than *that*.

"Go on, I said." She stamped her foot.

I was so hard-headed.

"Git! That toe'll get infected and you'll get *in-fan-tigo*."

I sauntered into the dark bathroom—half the time I never even pulled the long string for the overhead light. I opened up the medicine cabinet over the stationary wash stand, took out the bottle of peroxide, stuck my bare foot up on the toilet seat, and watched the cool clear liquid fizz over my toe.

~

When I was in fourth grade, Grandma's favorite sister, Alice, died of stomach cancer. They'd talked on the phone every day. After the funeral, something went out of Grandma. She complained of "swimming" in her head. She'd drag me along on the trolley to go to see Dr. McGinty.

We got on each other's nerves, especially in the dog days of August. As she got older, her disposition became as sour as her stomach. She took spoonfuls of Gastron and Hydrochloric acid to help her digestion. We played Rook so much we wore out the cards and always knew when the yellow ten was dealt.

Of course, I never realized how demanding a child I was, because I always felt sad inside, and I wanted my share of happiness too, even if it was just getting a drumstick over a fried chicken thigh.

I was so aggravating. More than once I drove Grandma to grab a coat hanger and chase me to the back bedroom and swat me, or reach over the banisters and break off a branch from the "bee bush" and strip it down and give me a switchin'.

I deserved all of them.

~

Chapter 7

Radio Days and Movie Stars

ON MONDAY EVENINGS I BEGGED MOTHER to let me stay up and listen to my favorite radio program: *Lux Radio Theatre*, a one-hour radio adaptation of the latest movies.

We slept at the foot of the bed because it was warmer and the radio was just behind us on the end of the dresser. As I lay under the heavy quilt with the light from the radio dial, I listened to the voice of—none other than—Cecil B. deMille, and real movie stars dramatically reading their parts.

There was such a shared intimacy lying there in the darkness next to Mother, wrapped within that "listening" experience—like a halo of hope—a promise that one day all that could be mine, too, if I could be in the movies.

I remember Olivia de Havilland's kind, gentle voice speaking right into my ear, as if she were there in my own bedroom. She paused . . . and sighed as she finished her sad story in *To Each His Own.* Tears trickled down onto my pillow.

For sheer listening pleasure, no radio voice matched raspy Mercedes McCambridge.

I can't remember ever missing an Academy Award broadcast on radio and later on television. I don't remember a time when I didn't want to win an Oscar.

And didn't Mother and I love *The Hit Parade!* If ever there was a program that defined our mother-daughter relationship, it was the excitement of guessing the hit song.

We huddled in the back-bedroom on Saturday nights, holding our breath, waiting to hear the number one song on the *Lucky Strike Hit Parade.* The drums would start rolling, the announcer dramatically broadcasting to all of America.

"And now, on the charts for sixteen weeks, the number one song is . . . "

I couldn't wait for each new issue of *Hit Parade Magazine* and learned the lyrics to my favorites: "Pistol Packin' Mama," "Swinging on a Star," and "Don't Fence Me In."

On days when it was cold or rainy, I stretched out on the double bed, surrounded by a growing collection of movie star photos which covered two walls as far as I could reach standing on the bed to pin them up.

~

Let me tell you about that tiny space that Mother and I made the best of for thirteen years. The room was maybe fifteen feet long and eight feet wide. A heavy door opened into the hallway. Everything was painted a washed-out blue, like someone had thinned down a leftover can of paint to cover the clapboard inside wall, all the beaverboard paneled walls, even the sloping beaverboard ceiling.

At the far end of the clapboard wall, someone had sawed an opening to access the bathroom and kitchen. I could take a flying leap from the doorway onto the bed because there *was no door.* Another opening was cut through to the kitchen. It was fitted with a short makeshift door that had a huge wooden spool nailed on it for a knob, making it look like a cottage door in a fairy tale about dwarfs. The bathroom was in between.

Grandma rarely came back there, so this space with the lumpy double bed was mine to have a temper tantrum, or suck my fingers and pout over not getting my way. There was already disappointment embedded in that mattress, along with the dust mites, so it was good to have a place for some hopes and dreams surrounded by Hollywood photos.

Each month I begged for fifteen cents to buy the latest copy of *Photoplay* or *Modern Screen*. I couldn't wait until the next day to run up to Setzer's Drug Store and buy one. Back home I would stretch out on the bed, hoping I'd be surprised and there would be a color photo of a star I really, *really* liked.

~

Miracle on 34th Street was especially memorable for me because little Natalie Wood's mother worked for Macy's and *my* mother worked for Rich's Department Store in Atlanta. Little Natalie was an only child living with her mother, and she didn't have a father, *either*.

How could any storyline be better than that!

But Natalie Wood and Maureen O'Hara lived in a gorgeous New York apartment and wore beautiful clothes, unlike Mother and me.

From then on I began fantasizing that Maureen O'Hara would adopt me. I would be her little girl and live in a beautiful house in Hollywood with her daughter Bronwyn. I had this guilty fantasy for years, along with fears that I might slip up and say something and give myself away. I worried about how much it would hurt Mother's feelings if she were to read my thoughts.

How could I dare to choose someone over Mother? How could I dare speak the truth, ever? Movies in which truth serum was injected frightened me.

Oh, but it was such a beautiful dream to have—to live in Hollywood with a beautiful movie star for a mother and have a sister, too.

I remember noticing how Lana Turner lifted her penciled eyebrow at a drifter who'd stopped in for coffee at this gas station lunch-counter. I knew she was interested in him, not that I would be—not even a cute drifter-type like John Garfield, because I already had my ideal: Dana Andrews or Cornel Wilde who played Chopin in *A Song to Remember*.

On the other hand, Betty Hutton exuded the kind of softhearted spunk that was most *like me*. In the movie *Incendiary Blonde*, she makes a passionate pledge to her poor family that she'll find a job and get the family back on its feet. And she does. But she falls in love with the wrong man.

When Betty Hutton sang "It Had to Be You," I felt all her heartbreak, and that song still melts my heart. The movie is listed as being released in 1945, so I must've been just eight or nine. Mother and I would have seen it together. Maybe I was really feeling Mother's melancholy that day.

~

If I'd had my 'druthers, though—more than anything I wanted to be a tap dancer. When I was seven, Mother took me to a Jack Epley tap recital. We sat in the balcony of the school auditorium, looking down at a young tap dance team, Sonny Cheatum and Tootsie Mitchum, a little Fred Astaire and Ginger Rogers couple. I loved them!

"Oh, Mother, that's what I want to do."

I squeezed her arm. "Look, Look!" pointing to their red, white, and blue, sparkly, sequined costumes, and Sonny in an adorable white top hat.

No amount of begging got me tap shoes or lessons.

~

In third grade, I envied my classmate Beverly Williams everytime she wore her beautiful soft white blouse and jodphers. I longed for my own pair. I was jealous of little Marilyn White who wore ruffled cotton panties, whose mother carefully curled her hair every day into adorable Shirley Temple curls, and who could already play "Butterflies" on the piano. Every time our principal, Miss Kendrick, called on little eight-year-old Marilyn to come up and play "Butterflies" before the entire school, I gnashed my teeth over her talent and the applause she received.

I wanted to shine, too, and when I overheard Mrs. Callaway, the other third-grade teacher say to my teacher, Mrs. Jenkins, "Charlotte's voice isn't good enough," referring to narrating the upcoming joint Christmas pageant, I never forgot it.

That's when I started changing my look.

I vividly remember the day of our school photo. I chose a nice dress, not one made of feedsack. I was seated at the end of the second row, my knees sticking out. I had on loafers and thin white socks folded over. At first, I had carefully arranged my Sunday dress over my knees. While the photographer was under his mysterious black cloth, adjusting his camera on a wooden tripod, I had time to think about the impending photo—that image—what someone might see me as—a young starlet, perhaps?

And so it was that in my third-grade photo I am no longer the grinning happy second grader wearing her victory badge, but a serious girl with simulated ringlets. Just before the shot, I eased my skirt up just enough to show my knees. I knew I shouldn't be parading my legs like that, but I'd seen Betty Grable sitting on the back of a jeep with her legs crossed. A snappy photographer had said, 'Hey, how about a little cheesecake?' and Betty Grable had smiled and pulled her skirt up just above her knees. Then the G.I.'s whistled, and flash bulbs popped.

(Mrs. Jenkins third grade class, 1945)

CAPTAIN MIDNIGHT

In good weather just before five o'clock you would find me balancing myself on my knees on the bed, carefully moving my little Emerson radio from the dresser to the windowsill to face outward. From there I would go outside and climb up the tall crape myrtle tree, seat myself in the fork of the sturdy, smooth limbs, and gently sway back and forth, high above the sloping backporch roof, reigning in kingly splendor, listening to: *The Green Hornet, Superman, Captain Midnight, Jack Armstrong* and *Sky King.*

"Stay tuned, boys and girls, for Captain Midnight's secret message!" said the announcer.

Oh, those enticing commercials.

"Boys and girls," continued the mellifluous voice of the narrator, "while you're decoding Captain Midnight's secret messages, you can sneak a glance in the mirror on your decoder badge to see if you're being detected!"

The ultimate lure of those ads was when the announcer said, "Boys and girls, set your Captain Midnight secret decoder badge for A-12."

And so would begin my suppertime campaign.

Mother was at the stove, spooning out some black-eyed peas and fresh cooked collards. She fished out the greasy piece of boiling bacon for her plate.

"Mother, can we please buy a jar of Ovaltine, so I can send off for Captain Midnight's decoder badge?"

I couldn't stand Ovaltine, and Mother knew it.

"You didn't drink up that last jar I bought," said Mother.

Every single day I didn't have a badge, I died of suspense. I listened to the numbers read so dramatically: "6, 3, 12, 12, 9," and all the while I was planning a new strategy for getting Mother to reconsider.

When I was least expecting it, Mother surprised me by bringing home the treasured jar of Ovaltine.

"Oh, thank you, thank you, Mother!" I shouted, hopping up and down, quietly hoping against hope that the flavor had changed, or that I had miraculously acquired a taste for malt. I was most anxious to prove my pledge to Mother, but even as I unscrewed the top and lifted the lid . . . *Oh no! That same smell!*

Even though I'd promised I'd drink it—it might as well have been castor oil.

"Well, this time, Shug, you can't have the label 'til you drink at least half the jar," said Mother.

The next afternoon I mixed up a glass and took three healthy sips, smacking my lips to try to make myself like it. No way. Then I sneaked out to the hall and poured it down a hole that went straight to the dirt below—the same hole where I had dropped crumpled Hershey wrappers. Peering down the hole, I wondered if there might not be some enormously healthy rats, or ancient super-spiders living off vitamin-enriched Ovaltine.

Eventually I hounded Mother into the label, but I felt guilty every time because I hadn't lived up to my word.

Since it was hopeless that I would ever acquire a taste for Ovaltine, I easily switched radio stations, changing my allegiance to Sky King and his sponsor, Peter Pan Peanut Butter, which I loved.

Before I climbed the crape myrtle, I often made a sandwich, spreading peanut butter on a piece of white bread to keep my nine round banana slices from slipping out on the ground. I tucked the sandwich inside my flannel shirt, then climbed to my perch high above the backporch for the daily radio adventures of Sky King, Penny and Skipper, and the whole bunch from the Flying Crown Ranch. They were like family.

I was so happy. Inside my head I was shouting:

"Look, look I'm one of you, up here in this tree, eating your Peter Pan Peanut Butter!"

When we didn't have bananas or peanut butter, I made plain ol' mayonnaise sandwiches, and once in a while I even made a catsup sandwich, but the bread got real soggy.

For fifty cents and a label I could send off for the amazing "Sky King Glow-in-the-Dark Ring."

Mother had her methods, too. She said I could earn fifty cents by memorizing Longfellow's *Daffodils,* which I did.

I sent off for the mail-order ring, then eagerly waited for the postman. Weeks and weeks went by. When I'd completely forgotten about getting my treasure, it arrived.

Amazingly, that Sky King ring was everything they said: a tiny ballpoint pen point was embedded in a piece of glow-in-the-dark plastic, and a hinge for the secret compartment. And to top it off, the ring was emblazoned with the Flying Crown Emblem.

Once I was dying for a mail-order device to show a movie on my very own wall, so I earned fifty cents by memorizing *The Gettysburg Address* from one of Mother's old school books since it was fairly short.

~

How wonderful to finally own a bicycle and ride to the Saturday movies. I would hop on and pedal away, get up enough speed to take my hands off the handle bars, then feel that joyous freedom of the wind in my face. At the movie theater, I parked and locked my bike and paid twelve cents for a ticket.

I loved smelling hot buttered popcorn as soon as I walked in the door of the Cascade Theater, then entering the darkness and feeling sticky floors as I found my way to a pull-down seat. Soon the movie projector was grinding away and the giggles and childish laughter began during the cartoon. I closed my eyes when the Mummy rose up out of his tomb.

My favorite cowboy was The Durango Kid, starring Charles Starrett in his all-black outfit, with his sidekick, Smiley Burnett. I loved to "play-like" the cowboy hero. Racing out of the latest cowboy adventure, my bicycle became my horse. I wished I didn't have to unlock it, so I could just leap on and pedal off as *The Durango Kid!*

"Come on, Smiley, let's get 'em!" I would say, kicking up the jack stand with a sharp blow, then pushing off with one foot on the pedal, commandingly swinging my leg over the seat as we galloped down Gordon Street chasing after rustlers.

There were plenty of male heroes but not many cowgirl stars. Dale Evans was always with Roy Rogers, but when trouble started, Dale would say, "Oh, Roy, I wanna go. Let me go, too!"

"No, Dale, you stay here. You might get hurt," Roy would say. "This is too dangerous for a woman."

I didn't want to be Dale Evans for that reason. She never got to save anyone. Just once I would've liked for ol' Dale to follow along behind Roy, wait until he was cornered, or tied up, and then bust in the back door with her cowgirl boot and fringy skirt and say, "Stick 'em up!" and rescue Roy and the gang and save the day.

But no-o-o! Dale had to stay back at the ranch and congratulate Roy on *his* bravery.

"Thank goodness you're back!" Dale would croon. "Oh, Roy, I was so worried. You're so brave."

~

The Saturday crowd at the Cascade Theater loved the Tarzan movies with Jane and Boy and Cheetah the Chimp. You never heard such cheering and stamping of little shoes when Cheetah foiled the Nazis.

An usher patrolling the aisles with a flashlight would shine it right in a child's face, muttering, "Pipe down, kid," if a child was too rambunctious.

In the middle of all our rowdiness, there was a sense of community—that joyful shared experience of childhood within the common boundary of neighborhoods and limits to which we knew we could safely go with our antics.

~

Chapter 8

Socializing the Heathen

IF THERE WAS SUCH A THING as a romantic tomboy, then that's what I was turning out to be, like Betty Hutton saying, "Gee Whiz" and "Dang it all!" and wanting to be a hero.

I remember the summer I decided to be Red Ryder's young sidekick, Little Beaver, who rode bareback and wore a quiver of arrows slung over his bare chest. I was about ten, I think, and went around in my long maroon corduroy pants with no shirt on. (They were my next favorite pair of pants.)

"Wha'cha wearin' them hot britches fer in this heat?" carped Grandma, seeing me rummaging in the kitchen drawer for some string.

"I'm playin' Red Ryder," I said, and then I just kept on going down the hall and out the back door to the back yard. I was about to make my very own bow and arrow. First, I stripped a branch from the althea bush, I think, or maybe a pussy willow limb. I notched the ends then wound a piece of string around each end, tying it off as taut as I could. I used another branch for an arrow, notched it, and tried to shoot it. Amazingly, those flimsy branches would actually fly a little ways—well, only when the arrow didn't stay stuck in the string. But I was proud of my effort. I enjoyed that endeavor as much as getting to shoot Lester's little store-bought bow and arrow set with rubber suction-cup arrows.

While I was dressed like Little Beaver, bare-chested with some watercolor marks across my nose, I walked up to the corner for some reason—maybe I had a nickel. A neighbor called Grandma and used the word 'heathen.' The story was retold over the front porch banisters in such a way that I felt like I had an invisible brand on me—H E A T H E N. I didn't understand. I didn't have breasts or anything, so I chalked up the word 'heathen' to being just another social boundary I'd bumped up against. Although, inside I cringed with shame over being an embarrassment to Mother who would soon enough hear about it.

I could not bear to disappoint Mother.

~

The Christmas Lester got a BB gun I just about died to shoot it. I never wanted anything so much in my life, except for a pair of cowboy boots, and a Flexy Racer—neither of which I ever got. Lester was my only playmate, an only child, three years younger than I. He lived on the other side of the Aldens in the brick duplex on the corner of Greenwich Street.

Every Christmas since they moved in, I couldn't wait to go see what he got because he would get everything I wanted, like Pound-a-Peg—which I practically wore out.

Over the years he got Tinker Toys, Lincoln Logs, and an Erector Set. What I loved was having someone to play with on their shiny waxed hardwood floor in their bright corner living room. I built forts with reddish grooved logs and showed Lester how to fit together the slotted Tinker Toy stick into a wooden circle.

Soon after Lester got his BB gun, Lester's daddy nailed up a target on the old carriage-barndoor at the back of their yard by the alley. I started being really nice to little Lester, who was about nine then. I even let him win at Chinese Checkers and tried hard not to be so bossy—like making him sheriff once in a while, instead of always my deputy. Lester wouldn't *ever* know the right things to say, so I'd have to tell him.

(Mother posing me and Lester in a shoot-out.)

"Les-ter, *you're* the Sheriff. Now, ya' gotta say, 'C'mon, let's round up a posse, and go get 'em.'"

I did finally get to shoot at the target and even learned to load the BBs that came in a little red cardboard cartridge.

Meanwhile, I continued to get gifts like a Bi-Lo Baby that wore a long embroidered gown. Whatever can you do with a baby? You can't even pretend a baby can talk.

'Goo-Goo!' That's all babies can say. Not, 'Stick 'em up!'

SMOKING AND THE MOVIES

Mother had once mentioned that boys in her day used to smoke rabbit tobacco in pipes made from acorns. I was curious to try out smoking because of the movies—like gangster movies where a detective, like Boston Blackie, had a cigarette hanging from his lips, suavely talking to the cops, or some dame.

Women were always dames in detective stories. I didn't want to be a dame though. I already wanted to have more class, be glamorous and maybe even elegant, like Merle Oberon.

I noted how Veronica Lake asked a man for a light, leaning in real close, so he could see how pretty she was. The smoke would be curling up as she held the cigarette with her wrist back between two glossy painted fingernails. Sometimes she would touch his hand as he gave her a light, to show he was special. Or a glamorous star would stamp out a cigarette she'd just lit up, crushing it into an ash tray, and say, "How dare you!" to emphasize that she was angry, but still a lady.

So, one summer I got this bright idea to fashion a pipe by hollowing out a fat acorn, using my small pocket knife which had only one tiny dull blade. I shortened the dried stem of a daylily for the pipe stem, wedging it into a tiny slit in the smooth brown shell.

Now what about tobacco? I'd noticed some cigarette butts on Greenwich, the side street by Lester's house, so I walked over and rummaged along the leaves in the gutter. I had just picked up a cigarette butt when Mrs. Morgan, who lived in the big white corner house across Greenwich, noticed me.

"Does your Grandmother know you're over here?"

I was immediately ashamed, just because of her tone.

"Uh-huh!" I nodded.

"Don't you know how to say, 'yes, ma'am?'"

I froze like a frightened animal and lowered my head, standing mutely, not wishing to be surly, but not wishing to tell the truth and admit I didn't know better.

It was a standoff, and she turned on her brown and white spectator pumps and walked back indoors.

Running home, I SLAMMED the back screen door, trounced up the hall and found Grandma listening to one of her favorite soap operas, *Our Gal Sunday.*

"Grandma, how come you don't ever teach me to say '*yes ma'am*,'" I demanded.

"You can by-God say it y'erself, if you want to. Hush up, I'm a' missin' what they'er' sayin'!"

The story that asks the question, 'Can this girl from a little mining town, find happiness as the wife of a rich and handsome Lord. Lord Henry Brenthrop.'

I picked my battles, and that wasn't one.

POISON IVY

Another summer I had a good project going, expecting to have so much fun with roofing strips and an entire sack of leftover roofing nails. I lugged a short roofing strip onto the back of the sloping garage and hoisted it up by standing on the garbage can.

I had dreams of repairing the sagging roof, but it hadn't turned out the way I thought. I couldn't seem to find the roof studs, and then I got scared that my nail pounding might actually make the roof cave in. I was still standing on the roof when I heard Grandma's second warning from the back door.

"I said, git down, that roof's a'sagging and you're gonna fall in!"

I hated to be defeated and yelled at to boot, but I climbed back down, balancing on the garbage can, and there I stood being disappointed over my roofing failure, standing right by the hairy vines of poison ivy growing on the back fence by the alley.

I'd been warned *not* to touch poison ivy, but that day I got the bright idea to see what would happen if I *did* touch it. So I took a big fresh, oily leaf between my palms and rubbed it back and forth, but good . . . waited a while . . . looked at my palms.

Nothing.

Then I went flying in the house, bursting into the kitchen where Grandma was at the stove.

I made my big announcement. "Guess what? I just rubbed poison ivy all over my hands!"

I held them up to show that nothing had happened.

"GOOD GOD A'MIGHTY! How could you do such a thing?" Grandma yanked me over to the kitchen sink where she turned on the cold water spigot and slapped the nasty brownish-yellow bar of Octagon soap in my palm.

"You jis' start scrubbin' those hands right now!"

Then she took the dishrag and soap and started rubbing my wrists and arms.

"You're gettin' a good switchin' for this!"

"But I didn't get it! I didn't GET poison ivy!" I screamed.

"By God, if you do git it, you'll by-God never touch it again," carped Grandma. "Elmer Hardaway's eyes swole up s'bad, he couldn't see. Calamine lotion didn't help him *one bit*, and they 'bout near had to put him in Egleston."

Luckily, I was spared the ravages of poison ivy.

And I'm sure I got a switching.

BUILDING A FLEXY RACER

More than anything I wanted a Flexy Racer—a sled with wheels. The store-bought ones, hanging up at Western Auto, were made of beautifully polished wooden slats. The front wheels had handlebars with rubber grips so you could turn left and right, and I'd imagined a beautiful dream ride on one of the super-duper models with hand brakes.

Bobby Blackwood's daddy had fashioned a homemade one for him. They lived way down the street somewhere. I got a good look at it one day from the sidewalk when he was pulling Bobby behind him to go to the store. He had made it out of scrap wood and attached a rope.

Whenever I saw Mr. Blackwood and Bobby, I thought of how wonderful it would be to have a daddy like him to make you a Flexy Racer, or some nice man like Mr. Sewell, our air-raid warden.

Flexy Racers weren't a practical toy for the city though. You had to ride them in the middle of a street with no traffic and a gentle slope.

But that made Greenwich Street perfect.

I was ten or eleven the summer I had the bright idea to build my own Flexy Racer. I used the side slats and wheels from my old wagon and some scrap wood in the garage which I cut the right lengths with the rusty keyhole saw some handy-man had left behind. But we didn't have any nails the right size, only roofing nails and some leftover finishing nails.

I'd noticed that our old sagging garage had nails that were loosening up just enough to get the claw hammer underneath the rusty nail head. The first one came out bent, but I kept at it, finding yet another loose nail and getting better and better, prying out more and more nails, slowly and carefully.

Grandma yelled from the back door, "Stop that! The garage is gonna fall down."

"Ok-a-a-Y!" I yelled back, sort of fussy-like, but I was thinking, *You don't know, it won't fall down.* I did worry that one night in a big winter storm, the garage *would* just collapse like a tired old dog, caving in on itself with its sagging roof and those missing nails.

After dismantling my old wagon I looked carefully to see how their wheels were attached. I discovered what a great invention a cotter-pin was—a little piece of metal that kept a wheel from falling off. Just as I was admiring it so, I dropped it in the weeds.

Dang! How could something go wrong so quickly?

I couldn't find it anywhere. I searched and searched, running my fingers through the weeds over and over. Then I remembered those leftover thin finishing nails, and I fashioned a cotter-pin by putting it through the hole in the wagon axle and pounding it back over.

The biggest problem now was how to attach the axle and wheels to the body.

I thought a big fence staple would be good, but we didn't have any. Then I thought maybe I could drive those longer garage nails in part way, and knock them back over, pounding the head in as deep as I could back into the wood. POUND! POUND! BANG! BANG! I did it! I had finished! I turned it over. It rolled! I was giddy with happiness. I attached a piece of old rope. My heart was bursting with pride.

I've done it, I've done it, I kept saying in my head as I pulled my homemade Flexy Racer across the yard to Greenwich Street to take my glorious ride.

If there'd been music, it would have been the sound of triumphant brass trumpets. I could've been any hero in a fairy tale that day, like Jack, victoriously bringing home the goose that laid golden eggs.

As I pulled my Flexy Racer off the curb, I was wondering if nosy Mrs. Morgan was looking at me out her kitchen window. I figured that when she saw what I'd invented—that this little girl had made her own Flexy Racer—she'd think better of me.

I put my invention right in the middle of the street, then lay down atop, holding it in place with my hands on the pavement. Then I let go. *Oh, I'm rolling!* It was so wonderful—for about two feet! The weight of my body had unbent the nails holding the axle. The whole contraption sagged and stopped.

Like Wilber and Orville on their first try, I had that one unforgettable, glorious moment. Then I dragged my precious invention back for improvements.

I must not've pounded those nails in good enough, I thought.

After a few more attempts, I gave up for the time being.

ELOCUTION

One night at supper when I was about twelve, I was sitting at the small kitchen table by the open window, the smell of the Aldens' fried pork chops drifting through the window. Mother was filling my plate from the stove—squash cooked with onions and fresh English peas with new potatoes.

It was always just the two of us eating supper. Grandma ate earlier from off the stove or at the side table, and then sat on the porch in summer, or sat in her rocker by the stove in winter listening to the radio.

"In my day children took elocution lessons," said Mother, as if she were making a point to someone in a conversation going on in her head. I didn't have any idea what had provoked that statement unless it was Grandma murdering the King's English again, or something came up at work.

I was busy skewering an ear of steamy boiled corn with two tiny yellow corn-cob holders, sticking them in either end. Mother filled her plate and sat down with the dishrag between us for the greasy drippings of boiling bacon the squash was cooked in.

"Elocution is part of being refined," she said, stuffing a small new potato in her mouth, chomping away.

"Refined, like refined sugar?" I said, adding fresh country butter and salt to my corn. I was getting to be a little bit of a "know it all." I'd noticed the word *refined* on the five-pound sack of Dixie Crystals sugar.

"Refined is acting nice," said Mother, slathering her own ear of corn with butter, which sat in a chipped saucer, "like you have manners and know what to say and do."

We didn't even *have* a dining room and never had any company, not even relatives.

Mother sank her teeth into her ear of corn, noisily going all the way down three rows like a typewriter, then chewing, swallowing, and starting back again on the next three rows.

"And in my day," Mother continued, "when we went visiting on Sunday, someone was likely to ask a child to give a speech. It was sort of expected."

"A speech!" I yelled, horrified.

Elocution sounded pretty boring to me and hard on a child. But those were the social graces of her day, even if they didn't get her out of her circumstances.

Being seen as refined was important to Mother.

"Well, not especially a speech," Mother continued, "just a little recitation or something." She started in on one of hers:

"*A birdie with a yellow bill/Hopped upon my window sill/ Cocked his shiny eye and said/Ain't you 'shame! You sleepy head!* Miss Molly McGee, my fifth-grade teacher, had us memorize that one." Then she laughed and said, "Don't evah say ain't! Ain't, *ain't* in the dictionary!"

Sometimes Mother could really get wound up when she got on the subject of bad English. She loved to repeat Grandma's misusage. "Mama al' time says, '*I seen 'im when he done it!*' and '*I taken,*' and '*he don't.*'"

She kept on imitating Grandma's mispronunciations, like *ernions,* for onions and *erunges* for oranges, till I was about to split my sides laughing. So maybe the subject of elocution *was* about something Grandma had said earlier.

~

Refined was one of Mother's favorite words. I think she had some running vision in her head from all those movies of what I might turn out to be. She wanted to offer me all the refinements she could afford, so she bought me one cultural book each year for a present, like *100 Best Loved Poems, Stories Behind the Great Operas* and eventually *The Complete Works of Shakespeare*, which I never read.

Often Mother took me to the children's section of the Carnegie Library. She read me books like *The Secret Garden*, The *Nicodemus* series, and *Miss Minerva and William Green Hill*, a series her teacher had read. Mother loved the part where Billy and his friend Jimmy put on blackface so they could take a trip on the 'scursion train.'

Years later I was saddened to realize how those authors used racial stereotyping to be humorous—sad, also, that Mother liked those stories so much.

I was proud to receive my first library card from the Uncle Remus Branch of the public library in West End. At the end of school I always wanted to show off by getting a summer reading certificate. I picked books that weren't too thick with lots of pictures. It seemed to me that if you earned a reading certificate, you counted for something, and that was a lot better than counting for nothing.

However, neither racial prejudice nor social grace seemed to sink into me too deeply.

And so it was, that one summer my two aunts decided it was their Christian duty to take turns at socializing me—I suppose because I was turning twelve in September.

Both of them lived across town with social connections as they say. Mother was always making fun of her cousin Clara, pointing out her high-falutin' manners.

"All Clara can talk about is 'the *U.D.C.* this, and the *D.A.R.* that,'" she'd say.

First, Aunt Gladys invited me to her house in Buckhead to attend a social etiquette class. I loved Aunt Gladys because she was so funny, made divinity, and did a great Br'er Rabbit dialect.

That summer she bought me a yellow organdy dress with a black vest that had black ribbons that crisscrossed in the front. It was the prettiest dress I'd ever had. I wore it with my black patent leather shoes to the etiquette class where a lot of gossipy ladies were listening to tips on etiquette.

When we got back to her house, Aunt Gladys had me practice walking around her living room with a book on my head. That was fun for a while since I had a good sense of balance and had once won a prize at a birthday party for balancing a potato on my head and walking around a coffee table more times than anyone else.

In the next etiquette class we practiced walking like a lady with one foot directly in front of the other. That exercise was awkward and unnatural, and I thought you really couldn't get to where you wanted to go by walking that way—which is the truth—unless, of course, you want to snag a Western Union lawyer like Aunt Gladys did.

THE UNITED DAUGHTERS OF THE CONFEDERACY

Not long after that week of etiquette, Grandma told me that Aunt Clara was coming by to start transporting me to weekly meetings of the United Daughters of the Confederacy. Clara was Aunt Alice's only child, a cousin once-removed, but I called her Aunt. She and Uncle Harry were well off and childless.

The day of the U.D.C. meeting, as it was called, Grandma said I had to get dressed up in socks and shoes. I picked out my aqua dress with big red and white flowers. I'd learned to tie my sash in back and I did so and then trounced into Grandma's bedroom to show myself.

"I got t' fix that hair," Grandma said, shouldering me back down onto her vanity bench, clamping me with her bony fingers.

"You jis' hold still."

She swatted my back with her big dirty white comb.

"And mind your Ps and Qs around all those fancy ladies and say 'thank you' to Clara when she brings you home."

Soon I was sliding into Aunt Clara's little gray coupe, feeling the scratchy upholstery on my bare legs. Aunt Clara was dressed in a white-collared, lavender voile dress, gray pumps, white gloves, and a gray straw hat with a bunch of tiny violets on the brim. I didn't *ever* get to ride in a car and I was very attentive, noticing how she shifted the gears with the earnestness of a missionary.

The U.D.C. meeting was held at a big assembly hall in an armory. I sat with other little girls and their sponsors, trying not to twist and catching myself if I banged my shoes on the rungs of the metal chair. My tight pigtails pulled my head with the rubber bands Grandma had put on the ends.

Perfumed ladies discussed projects they could drum up to expose us to the history of the War Between the States as it's known in the South. Then we young ladies were led over to a long table with a white tablecloth and a punchbowl at one end.

I didn't make friends with anyone, but stood in line watching what the others did. We were served pink punch in little glass cups and had to take a tiny scalloped napkin, find a place to sit, and eat a square of cake with a fork on a little plate.

I'd seen this in the movies, so I wasn't surprised, just uncomfortable. In the movies I was always rooting for the bumpkin who got invited to rich people's houses and then managed to shock and embarrass the fat hostess. But I didn't want to embarrass Aunt Clara in any way, not because of her, but because it would shame Mother. Well, no, I didn't want to shame Aunt Clara either, because I could see she meant well, and I did want to live up to her expectations, too.

The next U.D.C. meeting was held in *The Cyclorama* at Grant Park. *The Cyclorama* is a famous circular mural painting depicting General Sherman burning Atlanta to the ground.

Durn, I thought, *we're not even going to get to see that great painting,* because we headed down to the basement to study a huge black steam engine which loomed above us, guarded with a heavy maroon velvet rope, which let me know right away that getting to step up into the engineer's seat wasn't part of this excursion.

"Now girls," said Mrs. Abercrombie, our staunch U.D.C. leader, "this historic train engine was used in *Gone with the Wind,* and I hope this visit might inspire some of you girls to write a poem for your project, or do a pen or pencil sketch."

Project . . . we have to do a project?

I thought I might do a pencil sketch, if I had to, but then I'd have to stay there near the train for a long time with Aunt Clara.

Back home, as I was getting out of the car, I smiled nicely from relief.

"Thank you, Aunt Clara."

"Do you know what you'll do for your project?"

"No, ma'am."

By the next meeting, the same lady said, "Now, most of you have started on your project, and some of you have already completed yours. Those of you who haven't selected a poem or essay better get start-e-ed!"

I wish I'd never gotten into this.

"Remember, next week we will have our presen-ta-tions!" she said in a lilting voice, like this was the fun part.

Next week! Oh, no!

Another lady with dimpled hands and lots of rings stood up, clasping a lace handkerchief to her bosom and began to demonstrate in a swooning voice, *"Do-o-wn from the Hills of Ha-ber-sham-m-m, Do-o-wn From the Valleys of Hall-l-l!* Oh, what a lovely poem for someone to memorize, by Sid-ney La-nier! Georgia's State Poet." She swooned again, enticingly.

I racked my brain for some poem I already knew, or some picture I could trace out of a book, so I could get out of this easy, and not have to memorize *Marshes of Glynn* or *Song of the Chattahoochee.*

Then I thought of something . . . yes . . . something that would be really fine if not outstanding. Something I already knew. Aunt Clara was sitting across the room, all tense.

Oh, my idea seemed so good. I'll just raise my hand now and make my announcement. Yes, that'll be so great, and get me off the hook. My heart started beating. I could hear all the ladies saying, *Oo-oo-oo! Yes, how marvelous.* They would see how smart I was. I'd be discovered as some talented little genius from the "sticks," like in the movies. I raised my hand and stood up and proudly announced, "Aunt Clara, I know *The Gettysburg Address.*"

Oh, if there was ever a moment of restrained shock and horror—like 'Aunt Pittypat, bring on the smelling salts'—it was that quick *gasp*, almost in unison. And I thought the ladies were just flabbergasted that a little girl like me already knew *The Gettysburg Address*. I just kept standing there, hearing the murmurs, and finally someone with polite decorum said, "Some other time, perhaps, dear."

Then I was embarrassed, but I didn't know what was wrong, because I didn't know anything about *The Gettysburg Address* except that it was a famous speech by President Lincoln in Mother's old school book.

That turned out to be my last time at a meeting of the United Daughters of the Confederacy.

Fortunately, Aunt Clara stayed in good standing. She got so wound up in genealogy, she became eligible to be a member of the Daughters of the American Revolution and one day, years later, she sent me a letter to inform me I was eligible to be a Magna Carta Dame and my sons, Barons of Runnymede.

~

Chapter 9

The Holy Washrag

I REMEMBER THE SUNDAY MORNING it all started. Mrs. Cathcart, our stout, robust Sunday School leader, had just announced that our minister would be paying us a visit, when in walked Dr. Evans from the door behind us. Kay and I scrunched down in the long white pew. I ducked my head so as not to catch the eye of the minister, as I was sure the sole purpose of this ingratiating visit was to persuade those of us who hadn't been baptized to take the big plunge. I feared that—at eleven—we were the lone holdouts.

I could withstand the pointed parables about the perils of the unsaved, but the dreaded eye of the minister, magnified behind thick glasses, was to be avoided at all costs. No other eye—not even Mother's—put such a fear of God into me.

Anytime we stayed for church, we sat way up in the balcony where Dr. Evans could never catch your eye. But down here in this little Sunday School room with low ceilings, he loomed as large as God himself in a double-breasted navy blue suit.

Although Mother and Grandma belonged to the Gordon Street Baptist Church, they didn't talk much about the Bible or God. Mother had never put any pressure on me to join.

I nervously scraped my patent leather Sunday shoes under the pew, putting white scuff marks on my Vaseline shine. Dr Evans raised a solemn hand toward us, praising little George Henry Morgan for pledging his eight-year-old soul to Jesus three weeks ago.

Then he said, "Let us bow our heads and pray."

I sighed, bowing my head and closing my eyes for a moment, then picked at the scab on my knee, lifting up one hard, dried, crusty edge to reveal the tender pink skin underneath. I nudged Kay, hoping for an "Aar-r-g-g!" Kay didn't flinch.

The minister stretched out his arm, sweeping it grandly above our sea of shiny scrubbed faces bowed in prayer. He asked God for a blessing on us and said something about feeling the spirit and then did a quick left turn— as I suspected— onto the point I knew was coming. His voice then began to change to a mesmerizing tone, like a bumblebee quietly gathering honey.

"Now children, keep your heads bowed . . . eyes closed. Children . . . those of you who *haven't* joined the church, would you raise your hands?"

A heathen, yes! A liar, no! I raised my hand.

"Now children . . . keeping your eyes closed . . . raise your hands if during the next week, you will just *think* about giving your life to Jesus."

No way would I raise my hand this time. Not on your life! This was spiritual harassment.

I did not relish joining the church at all. For one thing, I was afraid of some unknown commitment to *being* or *becoming* something I wasn't ready for. For another, I harbored a secret fear I might be asked to give up something I treasured—some kind of proof of my commitment—like giving up Hershey bars.

Now if the minister had asked me to commit myself to becoming a movie star, I would've run down the aisle of the

Gordon Street Baptist Church and dropped to my knees, pledging to work myself to the bone, studying, sacrificing, doing anything, because that's where my heart was.

My heart wasn't with Jesus; it was with show business.

I'd been known to lounge on the sagging double bed in the back bedroom eating banana sandwiches, reliving the last movie Mother and I had seen, staring at movie star photos pinned all over the walls. If the movie was a musical, I dreamed of being a tap dancer or night club singer. After *Singing In the Rain*, I grabbed the first pole I saw on Gordon Street to try to swing on it like Gene Kelly. If the heroine was jilted, I relived her sadness, replaying the scenes, sighing, crying and dying with all those Hollywood legends.

~

It was summer vacation and I'd invited Kay to bring her comics to my house. We were sprawled out on the iron daybed that had been moved by the long, open window on the back porch on the other side of the house—the coolest place in summer. That room was locked off from the tenants, serving mostly as a junk room and housing the water heater.

In between swapping comic books I started up a conversation.

"Kay, do you think we're the only two girls that haven't joined the church?"

"Uh-huh."

"No, really, Kay."

"Uh-huh. We are."

"How 'bout Betty Ann Grove?"

"She doesn't hardly ever come to Sunday School. That doesn't count."

"What about the Cagle twins?"

"They joined already."

"The Cagle twins joined?"

"You missed that Sunday."

"*Durn!* We *are* the last."

Now we were stuck. I swapped Kay a *Wonder Woman*, which was originally hers, for a *Betty and Veronica*, which was originally mine.

Then I asked, "Well, did you ask your mother about joining?"

"Uh-huh."

"Wha'd she say?"

"I can do whatever I want."

"Me too. Mother doesn't care, either."

Silently we thumbed through more pages. Finally the torment was just too much for me.

"Listen Kay, let's just join together next Sunday. Okay?"

"Uh-huh."

It was such a relief to have made that conspiratorial decision. However, that started an even greater agony of going through with it.

The following Sunday I wore my favorite dress, a pale blue, pink, and purple plaid with a little white collar and a thin black velvet string bow. Kay was in her green and white dotted Swiss with a white collar.

We sat downstairs on the third row on the left side because nobody we saw ever joined from the balcony. After the sermon Dr. Evans announced the invitational hymn. The congregation rose. After the organist played the introduction, we solemnly began singing *"Just As I Am."*

Neither Kay nor I moved a hair. We stood like zombies, holding onto the Baptist Hymnal for dear life, a frozen hand on either side, not daring to look up, or at each other, throughout the entire six verses, secretly hoping the other wouldn't step out.

After church, we laughed with relief.

"How come *you* didn't go?"

"How come *you* didn't?"

"Okay, next week!"

And we did. The following Sunday, as soon as the invitational hymn began, we slipped out of the same pew and walked to the front of the church. Dr. Evans put out his big fat, warm hand and took my small one, though I carefully avoided his eye, afraid he would see my doubt. The congregation fervently sang on as Kay and I stood huddled together. You could feel the audience smiling, and sense they were elbowing each other.

"That's Margaret Ashurst's little girl, isn't it?"

"And who's that with her? The Tallant girl? Her name's Kay, I think."

We got lots of handshakes and shoulder pats. Members who had never spoken to us before clamored over us like we had just finished swimming the English Channel. We smiled and basked in the short-lived attention, for now we had to be baptized.

Neither of us had learned to swim, adding to our fear.

George Henry Morgan was to be baptized that night, so we decided to go and watch. We sat up in the balcony and anxiously waited for the baptisms to begin. We had to listen to extra singing and a short sermon, then more singing as Dr. Evans left the pulpit, soon to mysteriously appear in the baptismal pit above the choir loft.

I was hoping little George Henry might just choke and drown and wouldn't that be something? Maybe then they'd just call off all baptisms.

Soon the lights were turned off, and just above the choir loft, a spotlight appeared on the curtains. They magically opened, revealing the baptismal chamber where Dr. Evans appeared wearing a black robe.

Mrs. Vickery played ever so softly on the piano. There was such a solemn feeling as the minister sloshed over to the first baptizee, who was offstage, so to speak, and led him through the water, centering him near the front. Then he covered his face with the holy washrag.

I got the holy washrag idea because Mother always covered my face with a washrag when she ducked me backwards in the bathtub to rinse the shampoo out of my hair. I screamed bloody murder if any suds or water whatsoever got in my eyes. Having my hair washed in the kitchen sink was an even bigger ordeal I fought every time, and consequently, I went around with a lot of tangled and dirty hair.

I noticed Dr. Evans had a little cheat-sheet up in back, because he waded upstream in between dunkings to read the next name which turned out to be Mr. Steckel, a heavyset Methodist transplant who married the widow Echols. I nudged Kay, suspensefully, waiting to see if Mr. Steckel just might not take the minister down with him.

"Edward Foster Steckel, I baptize you in the name of the Father, the Son . . .," — the holy washrag went over his nose, and then a quick, skillful dunking, if I do say so, myself, just as the minister was saying, ". . . and the Holy Ghost."

Mr. Steckel came up sputtering.

Next, Dr. Evans waded out holding up little George Henry with his head just peeking above the water so we could see him. As he was ducked under, his little feet popped up, but he didn't whimper.

"Durn!" I muttered to Kay, seeing him take his baptism like a little man.

The following Sunday, Mrs. Andrews, our Sunday School teacher, told us how proud she was we had decided to take Jesus Christ as our Lord and Savior and then informed us that we had to have an interview with the minister— alone!

Oh, ye gods! The eye of the minister! If I'd known that was part of the deal, I would've never joined. I'm sure no one mentioned this interview on purpose.

~

It was late summer, time for my interview. How I'd managed to postpone that dreaded visit was amazing. First, I stubbed a toe, then I had a mosquito bite that happily led to impetigo, then Dr. Evans went back to Wales, where he was born, for his vacation. I hoped he might decide to stay.

As I dawdled the ten long blocks to the church, everything along the way captured my attention. I stopped to press my finger on a low hanging mimosa frond to '*make it go to sleep.*' Then I noticed a bee buzzing in the center of a purple althea blossom. Its little yellow-coated feet suddenly held great interest.

As the sidewalk crossed over the railroad overpass, I noticed the fast growing kudzu twining along the wrought-iron railing. A similar vine entwined itself with equal vigor from the other side. I wondered, as I did every year, if the two vines would meet in the center before frost.

Finally, I found myself in the minister's office, sitting in a polished oak chair by his desk, my head down, avoiding his eye. I was sure he was about to say, *'To become a Christian you must be willing to give up . . . '*

I was prepared to lie and say I'd give up "Raisinettes" because I hated raisins.

But instead he said, "Charlotte, do you know what it means to be Christian?"

That was even worse because I had no idea.

Because he was from Wales, he pronounced my name with a *Ch* instead of *Sh*, and it made me feel like he didn't know who I was. Like maybe *I* was the foreigner—which in a way I was.

I took a deep breath and said, "It's where you say . . . you say . . . er, you believe in Jesus . . . and . . .um . . . try to be good all the time . . . and then your face is covered with a holy washrag and you get baptized in this sacred water."

He said the water wasn't sacred, just plain old water, the same as came out of my kitchen sink.

What? I thought. *It's not special water, dyed blue or something?*

I was pretty disillusioned after that. But he didn't say anything about the holy washrag and continued on with his message of scary dutiful things about being a Christian. So I figured I better just let it go at that.

Oh, Lord, was I ever glad to get out of that office. I had a greater appreciation for all the suffering Jesus did on the cross.

I walked home crossing back over the overpass, stopping to lean over the wrought-iron rail—looking down the long, lonely tracks. President Roosevelt's dead body, in a special funeral car, had travelled those tracks from Warm Springs to Washington. I wished I could've been one of those people I saw in the newsreel crying and waving the American flag all at the same time. President Roosevelt's death had been like losing God, and those tracks were sacred to me.

I sat down on the warm pavement dangling my legs over the edge, pressing my face between two warm metal railings. I'd hoped there was something special about this baptism ritual that I didn't know about. Secretly, I was waiting for some magic awakening inside.

Maybe it would come *after* I was baptized.

Kay and I learned the next Sunday morning that we were to bring an extra pair of underpants for our baptism that night, which made us even more scared and giggly.

During the evening church service Kay and I slowly walked up the back steps to a little dressing room where some fussy church ladies helped us get into white cotton robes, then lined us up in the order of our dunking. The first thing I noticed was that Dr. Evans had on these big black rubber hip boots.

So, that's how he gets back downstairs so quickly, all dressed back in his preaching suit!

I waited nervously in line, glad Kay was behind me clutching my robe. Then it was my turn. Dr. Evans took my hand, and I sloshed down two tile steps with Kay still holding onto my robe . . . then she finally let go.

I waded into the water, looking out into the darkness of the sanctuary where I knew Mother was sitting. I saw dust particles and a moth flutter in the stream of light beaming straight into my eyes. Little waves of warmish water slapped at my chin. As Dr. Evans adjusted his hand on my back, I heard Mother clearing her throat way out in the hushed congregation, and I wondered if she was going to cry. The minister covered my face with the holy washrag, said the magic words, "In the name of the Father, the Son, and the Holy Ghost," and ducked me under. I sputtered, but I didn't drown. He gave me a little shove to get me going upstream, and the church ladies dragged my soaking body up the steps. Oh, Lord Jesus, was I ever glad that was over with.

Now I am a Christian, I mused with wonder.

I waited two weeks to see if I was going to change in any way, like with my vaccination scab which left a permanent scar. I thought perhaps my sincerity in wanting to be better, now that I hadn't been asked to sacrifice Hershey bars, might make me the one person in the church that was significantly changed.

I did love Jesus's attitude, how he loved ALL the little children, *'red and yellow, black and white,'* when nobody in *my* neighborhood, or anywhere else I knew, talked kindly about any colored people, unless they were in *Gone with the Wind.*

~

In two weeks of hot Georgia sun, the kudzu had grown almost twelve feet from each end of the overpass bridge.

Maybe this year the vines will meet in the middle, I speculated, hanging over the railing again. The kudzu had covered all the trees with huge fuzzy, fig-shaped leaves looming like giant prehistoric creatures. The tough vines dauntlessly crept down the embankment and onto the tracks where their relentless growth was thwarted daily by rattling trains.

I pondered my baptism—I mean, this change was what it was all about, wasn't it? Though I never saw any transformation in a single person in my church. Ever.

What was to become of me? I wondered. Would I one day ride down those same tracks and become someone special? Or would I be like that kudzu vine—that never belonged in Georgia in the first place—that knew only that it wanted to grow into becoming itself, yet cut back daily by a rattling train.

Baptism was another of many illusions I was to pass through on my journey to personhood.

~

Chapter 10

The King of Hearts

MOTHER HAD JUST COME HOME FROM WORK. I was dying to tell her about our new song-flute ensemble and a new boy who had transferred to our fifth grade class.

I was sprawled out on the double bed waiting for just the right moment. I practically lived in that bed. Mother was always reminding me, 'That's a Beautyrest mattress,' as if that redeeming brand name would make up for the lumps and the rancid smell.

I watched while she undressed in front of the yellowed dresser mirror, changing out of a dark green belted gabardine dress, standing there in a plain white rayon slip, telling a story about the girls in the office. I was saying *uh-huh*, or laughing if she said something funny. She unpinned her underarm dress shields, and I knew she'd rinse them out and use them again tomorrow in a different dress.

Since there was no closet, we hung our clothes on an aluminum hanger that fit over the heavy door to the hall. After that the door never shut completely.

If anything got broken or unhinged, it stayed like that from then on, just like our lives.

Mother slid open a space and hung hers there, behind my three school dresses and one Sunday dress. She would wear it again in three days. Pulling off her rubbery girdle, she picked up her cotton print dress thrown over the 20s radio bench, then she breathed in the freedom of loose clothes, happy to be home from adding up invoices at Mutual of Omaha.

And now was the right moment.

"The music teacher wants me to play a duet with Robert," I said. "Can I have a dollar for a song flute?"

I knew before she said it, what she was going to say.

"Do I know Robert?" Mother asked.

"He's the new boy. Real smart. Plays the trombone and they live on Allegheny, near White Street," I said scared to be talking about him. "And he's an only child, like me."

"Allegheny, huh!" said Mother, recognizing a newer section, better than ours.

I'd never been interested in a boy before, but I had my ideals from the movies. Other boys had given me Valentines, but none had seemed like such a good match.

For one thing, Robert was second in math for the boys, and I was second in math for the girls. Well, maybe I was third; Jeanette and Grace were smarter, but Mrs. Gilmer, our red-headed teacher, had put Robert and me together several times to go to the board for the math relay. And mostly he won, but sometimes I won, and it felt good to win, but I needed a worthy opponent. And Robert was worthy though not what you would call handsome. He had straight brown hair, neatly parted, and his Mother dressed him in sweater vests.

~

Mother did buy me that song flute, and I practiced long and hard. There we were, two ten-year-olds that fate had put together, playing a duet of "Country Gardens." It was just like the movies! Mother had gotten off work and sat smiling and clapping out in that sea of parents sitting on wooden folding chairs in the school auditorium.

All I wanted that day was to *not* make a mistake and make Mother smile. The children's applause was fun, too.

~

I wanted to learn to play a real instrument *so bad* as we say, especially because Robert already played the trombone. It was the best new dream in the world.

I told Mother the school band leader said I could play a clarinet. She said we couldn't afford the lessons, or the rental, so that stopped that as we also say.

Then one day Mrs. Guy, our weekly music teacher, brought in a ukelele. I loved it! I asked her to show me how to play the two chords to "Polly Wolly Doodle." I practiced until I knew it. It felt so good to learn something by myself, something to entertain myself with, except I didn't yet own a ukelele.

Next, Mrs. Guy chose some of us to learn two-part harmony. I loved hearing the sound of two voices, each singing their own note, but in harmony. And a two-part harmony was what Robert and I were becoming, because Mrs. Gilmer planned a school play and selected Robert and me to have the main parts as Peace and Discord.

I couldn't believe she picked me, and I couldn't help but look at Robert with even more admiration. We were the *chosen* ones, just like a fairy tale or central casting. Every afternoon back home alone stretched out on the bed, I read over my lines. I had something to live for.

The afternoon of our play the school auditorium was noisily filling with other classes. Backstage I noticed my throat getting dry and my stomach clenching up. I so wanted to do a good job. As I moved out from behind the long, heavy velour curtain, my hands were cold; I felt both scared and brave. Then I took my place on one side of the stage as Peace, with Robert on the other side as Discord, and the performance began. I had to say all these *goody-goody-two-shoes* lines while Robert got all the laughs as Discord. Even so, I liked being on stage and the applause.

∼

In the spring Mrs. Gilmer put Robert and me in charge of the Friday afternoon movies. After our short training period our teacher just left. Robert loaded the film and started the movie projector. I filled out the forms and turned off the lights, and we sat on the back row by the projector, and . . . I don't know how it started . . . but soon we began holding hands. I remember spreading out my cotton skirt in case anyone suddenly opened the door.

A romantic movie scenario was already unfolding for me. On those Fridays I held the power of a ten-year-old impresario, knowing the films ahead of time, bossing the class a little bit while anticipating back-row pleasure. I remember the touch of Robert's hand in mine, feeling capable, warm, and sensual—so compelling and quietly exciting—like nothing I'd ever felt before. I can still feel the warmth it caused, like melting lava inside my stomach.

On the last day of fifth grade Mrs. Gilmer announced she was moving up to be our sixth grade teacher. We all clapped and cheered. Oh, happiness, indeed, to stay with our same friends. And Robert and I would be in the same room again.

In sixth grade Mrs. Gilmer chose a more elaborate play, *The Queen of Hearts.* She selected Robert and me for the king and queen. I love the photo of the entire sixth-grade class in costume, spread out across the school stage. Some of the girls wore big paper hearts tied on their heads. Robert and I wore white paper crowns with little red hearts glued on the points. I had on a long dress with white netting. Robert wore a cape, and we held hands at the end of the play.

All I wanted *next* was to keep on holding hands with Robert and still make Mother smile.

∼

(Mrs. Gilmer's sixth grade class play, 1946)

That spring Mrs. Guy taught us to waltz and fox trot. Every Wednesday afternoon Joseph, the janitor, put all the auditorium chairs around the edge of the hardwood floor.

Step-together-step. Step-together-step.

I learned the dance steps with my regular partner, Gordon Woods, because we were the same height. But whenever we got a free dance, Robert always asked me.

I'm remembering a song now, "Dance, Ballerina, Dance," a popular waltz Mrs. Guy played on her phonograph. On those afternoons the orchestra music changed the auditorium into a special realm, a magic ballroom with long windows and the heavy maroon velour curtains with gold fringe across the stage.

I remember the feel of Robert's thick hand in mine and the other one pressing firmly into the small of my back. My hand was resting on his shoulder, feeling his muscles beneath his sweater vest or plaid shirt.

After many weeks we had a ballroom dance performance. The parents sat in the wooden chairs around the walls. Mrs. Gilmer lined us up in the hallway two by two, shirts tucked in, hair bows straight. Mrs. Guy put the needle down on the record and in we danced with our partner, sliding stiffly in our Oxfords and loafers—*step-together-step*—to the sounds of saxophones, trombones, and clarinets.

SATURDAY MOVIES

Soon Robert and I met at the Saturday movies.

I rode my blue bicycle, wearing my favorite outfit: rolled up blue jeans, a red-and-brown flannel shirt, and Dan Cohen brown high-top tennis shoes with little airplane treads on the bottoms. I bought a twelve-cent ticket, a box of popcorn, and a Hershey bar with almonds and waited nervously excited for the feel of Robert's hand. We sat on the fifth row from the back where we watched a serial, a cartoon, and a cowboy or gangster movie.

That was probably the happiest time of my life, the freedom of a bicycle, being a good student with enough money for the Saturday movies, feeling chosen, and especially having another only child to feel close to.

We were sweethearts and belonged together and nothing had gone wrong—so far.

But then I made a fatal mistake.

One Saturday during a scary movie, I felt a compelling urge to put my arm around Robert's shoulder. I don't know what made me want to be so bold. I knew I was doing a daring thing. Even though he was a boy, I felt tender and protective of Robert, like I was being his mother more than a sweetheart.

The next Monday a girl came up to me in the girls' bathroom and asked me, "Did you really put your arm around Robert?"

Then another girl chimed in and said, "Girls aren't supposed to do that!"

I turned beet red, ashamed, feeling like some hussy in the movies. As soon as I got home, I lay on the bed and cried silently so Grandma wouldn't hear me. And I was never that bold again.

Then sixth grade was over.

I had mixed feelings about moving up to seventh grade. What would it be like? Would I still make good grades in this last year of grade school?

And especially, would Robert be in my class?

~

SEVENTH GRADE

Walking to school, that first day of seventh grade, crossing over the railroad overpass, looking down the tracks, I was hoping that I'd be selected as a safety patrol girl with a white belt and badge, and maybe even get to go to Washington, D.C. I dreamed of what it would be like to be on a train with other patrols, chugging out of my home state to see the U.S. Capitol, the Washington Monument, and maybe meet President Truman.

What an awful disappointment seventh grade turned out to be. Some of the boys were taller than our teacher Miss Frances Carson. Some girls had started wearing brassieres. I was wary of a new boy, Jack, tall and surly with long hair hanging over his eyes. I imagined him to be a juvenile delinquent, winding up in reform school, terms I'd learned from the recent movies.

I was selected to be a safety patrol, but there were no plays or fun activities in Miss Carson's strict teaching methods. The only project I liked was coloring in the countries of South America on a blank map and writing in the capitols.

A new boy named Jim, sat next to me and had body odor. After a sweaty recess I could hardly bear his smell. One hot afternoon during a class discussion, Jim turned to me and said, "I'm an atheist." *Lord!* I didn't know what to think. He seemed like a fat little alien.

Someone in the girls' bathroom reported hearing about a sex act in the boys' bathroom. *Yikes.* I didn't want to hear of such things within the halls of my beloved J.C. Harris school.

I still noticed what Robert wore, and how he answered any question the teacher asked him. During the summer he'd invited me to go with his parents to see Guy Lombardo's orchestra and an Atlanta Cracker's baseball game.

I'd also heard about a new girl in town in the other seventh grade class, and one spring day in the girls' bathroom, a loud-mouthed girl named Anne, said, "Robert likes Judith Foster *better* than *you!*"

What! I was stunned. I had taken our being sweethearts for granted.

I'm sure I covered up my shock that day by acting nonchalantly. I remember leaning over the wash basin rinsing my hands over and over like Lady Macbeth, hoping I could make the bad news go away.

After everyone had left, I just stood there numb in the coolness of the girls' bathroom, looking over at those silent marble slabs around the toilet stalls, feeling like I might throw up.

All I wanted to do was go home and die.

Those words, "Robert likes Judith Foster *better* than *you*!" had torn right through my heart. I came home hurting like it would never stop.

I quietly eased open the back door and went straight into the back bedroom so Grandma wouldn't hear me. I lay on the bed furious at Anne, the 'bathroom messenger.'

I turned on the radio and the song "My Foolish Heart" was playing. It was so beautiful and sad, and I'd just seen the movie and loved it.

Tears came in my eyes as I began remembering the movie. In the movie Susan Hayward is madly in love with Dana Andrews, but he's killed in the war and leaves her pregnant. She marries someone she doesn't love and tries to be happy, but she drinks a lot and invites her college girlfriend over to talk about when she first fell in love. She keeps filling up her glass with scotch, and all that time the song is playing *"Beware, my foolish heart . . ."*

You know how it is—you start feeling so sad for Susan Hayward and you start crying. You replay the movie in your head. She's lost Dana Andrews and she's *never, ever* going to be happy for the rest of her life, and now she's made this huge mistake of, not only getting pregnant, but also, marrying someone she doesn't love. But then you realize *you* have those *same feelings,* and the shock is awful. You don't want to be vulnerable and, moreover, you didn't *even know* you loved Robert the same way Susan Hayward loved Dana Andrews. All those feelings were spilling out.

Robert is gone and never coming back.

I cried for so long my bones ached. I never told anyone.

Who would understand, anyway?

I vowed to seal off all my feelings. If I never cared or let myself be vulnerable, I'd never have to feel the pain. And I did. I taped up that gaping hole with childish psychic cellophane tape.

~

Near the end of school all the city safety patrols were invied to a live Saturday morning performance of The Three Stooges in person at The Erlanger Theater.

I was so thrilled.

The night before, I scrubbed my patrol belt with an old toothbrush and Ivory soap. I felt so special to meet up with Robert that morning and we sat together, but neither of us reached for the other's hand.

Still it was exciting to sit with other city patrols hearing the laughter and cheering the noisy antics of Moe, Larry and Curly in person.

I remember Robert and I walking out together through the Erlanger theater lobby with the coming-attractions movie posters in glass frames along the sides. I had a lump in my throat, but I got up enough nerve to say, "Anne said you like Judith Foster better than me."

He hesitated.

We kept on walking.

"I don't know," he said.

I knew it was over.

I had dreamed of the safety patrol train trip to Washington, D.C., but when it came time for the tickets, Mother said, "We can't afford it."

At the end of the school year, we turned in our patrol belts and shook hands with our teacher.

In the fall we would become eighth graders at Brown High School.

My beloved grade school would be left behind. The innocence and beauty and Robert, too, were gone forever.

~

THE SUMMER OF '49

I was completely disillusioned about romantic love. Inside was an emptiness, and now I was beginning to feel the allure of sexual attention. Thus began a disturbing summer.

It began on a cinder-covered area in front of the old carriage barn in Lester's backyard where his father had put up an orange basketball hoop. Lester and I were awkwardly learning to dribble and shoot. That's when Carl Martin and red-headed G.W. Heard started hanging around wanting to play, too.

I started rolling my shorts up, wearing Mother's soft yellow knit shirt. I did this because I'd seen older girls at the swimming pools dressed like that. It went against all my natural instincts, but still I did it.

That summer a boy named Ben, who had been in school with me since second grade, talked himself into our tiny living room where we sat on the horsehair divan and leafed through the *Sears & Roebuck* catalog together.

Don't ask me how that got started. I have no idea!

When we got to the corsets and brassieres section, Ben started breathing heavily, and I wondered what on earth was the matter with him. Then he lunged at me trying to embrace me. I felt his soft, fuzzy, hot cheek next to mine for only a moment, noticing the light mustache hairs that would soon need shaving. I wanted no part of this. He was too big, too heavy, too aggressive. I pushed him away and out the door.

But the next week, he was back at the front door like a stray cat that forgot it was shooed away, and I unhooked the screen door, again, when he suggested looking at the Sears catalog again.

I knew better.

I didn't even *want* this to be happening, but I must've been nuts, or too compliant to have the courage to say no.

This time I handed *him* the catalog; I took the piano stool, still wearing shorts. And this time, when he got to the corsets and underwear section, he lunged at me again, and got his hand under my shirt and onto my white cotton bra before I could push his sweaty body off and shove him out the door again.

"And don't do that anymore," I said. And meant it. And he didn't come back.

That summer I started my period. Even though I'd seen Mother in a sanitary belt practically every month of my life, and even seen blood on the sheets, it was a shock to see my own blood. When Mother bought me a Kotex belt, I was not happy about it at all. Aunt Gladys got on the phone with me and tried to explain some kind of jabber about 'now you're a woman,' which I couldn't care less about.

Very inconvenient, in my opinion.

A LATER DREAM

Years later, in my forties, I had a dream which opened in that same dark basketball court area, with those crunchy gray, other-world cinders.

Each scene of that dream—and there were seven—went back in time: scenes of communal rituals of birth, healing, women washing clothes by a riverbank, burials, women by a fire pit. In the final dream scene, I am in a deep cave with an old woman wearing a dark pointed hood, sitting in a yellowish light.

I call this *the knowing cave where the bones reside*—that base of instinctual knowledge all women have.

Even though I was learning how to be a woman from copying stuff in the movies, I realize, now, that there were deeper intuitive signals going on—messages that belonged just to me—something I had to decode on my own—in the context of my generation, in order to learn what kind of woman I wanted to grow into.

~

Summer was over. I'd been looking forward to high school for so long, yearning to be like the older girls with notebooks, wool skirts, sweaters, wearing a boy's football jacket.

But high school was nothing like I'd imagined.

~

Chapter 11

Eighth Grade Madness

I HAD BARELY TURNED THIRTEEN when I entered an overcrowded high school with 1,500 students. The first morning Miss Andrews, our eighth grade homeroom teacher, passed out our class schedules. I didn't even know where the stairwells were. Then she passed out our locks and locker number assignments, warning, "Do not tell *anyone* your locker combination, and *do not* write your number above your locker."

A bell rang.

We had only five minutes between classes.

The noisy hallway was chaotic with students jammed in on either side of me. I put my notebook and lunch down on the hall floor to get the combination exactly right, fumbling with the heavy lock and turning the dial, sweating and feeling like the most inadequate person ever.

Someone exclaimed, "Yay!" And a metal door banged opened against my ear. Someone else pointed me the way up a flight of stairs to my first class, Health Science. It wasn't a room at all—not even any desks. We just stood around in a narrow room lined with trash cans off the cafeteria. Our teacher said his name was Coach Rowlett.

A coach for a teacher? I was so confused. *What is this high school madness?*

I hated not knowing what to do. I hated feeling lost. I hated that I felt more alone than ever, and there were no friends and no one to ask. I tried to keep a grip on my nerves.

Coach Rowlett was tall and thin, with very even, white teeth and a genuine smile. He said he was the Brown High basketball coach. He reassured us that this room was temporary and that tomorrow we would be in our regular classroom. I didn't feel reassured at all. I had never heard a term like Health Science and had no idea what kind of class I had been assigned.

The hallway was packed with students between classes. I hated passing the big boys with their loud mouths and roughness —not all the boys, of course, but the swaggering-types. I saw one boy getting "fresh," with a girl whose locker was next to his, and I knew to be wary. Sometimes I'd catch a glance of someone from my old J. C. Harris grade school, nodding or smiling at me, but their face would disappear into the rushing crowd.

I was already worrying that I'd never get my locker back open again. I worried that if I didn't, I'd never tell anyone and go hungry at lunch time. I had made a pimiento cheese sandwich and some Ritz crackers with peanut butter wrapped in waxed paper, and suddenly it was the only thing I was looking forward to.

This is the worst day of my life, I kept thinking. *How will I manage?*

Next I had a horrible English class with Mrs. Castello, who assigned us homework the very first day.

"Conjugate the verb *to be*," she said.

Maybe she wrote something on the board about verbs that day, but I must've missed that part. I'd never heard that term, *conjugate*.

I came home totally frustrated and went straight to the back bedroom to look up the word *conjugate* in the dictionary and try to figure it out. I'd been waiting my whole life for high school and here I wasn't even able to do my homework!

Grandma was sick most of the time now, and I didn't want to be a bother. She had a practical nurse during the day, Mrs. Blake, who cooked heavy biscuits with flour on the tops.

I lay on the bed, wrestling over, *I am? you is? he is? No. That can't be right.* I knew "you is" was dialect.

Trial and error. Story of my life.

Why was I like that?

I do know I didn't ever want to look stupid or lose face by not knowing something. I think I felt like I was supposed to figure out everything on my own.

Lord! I analyze too much.

I did turn in my homework. It was nearly right, so I didn't feel as bad as I thought I would.

A GENERATION ENDS

I woke up hearing Grandma calling from her bedroom, "Tot-sy! Tot-sy!"

Mother heaved a sigh, her body tense. I felt Mother's thin batiste nightgown sticking to her damp body. It was a muggy night, moonlight streaking across our bed from the small open window.

"Tot-sy-y-y! Tot-sy-y-y!" Then we heard a long scream. Mother jumped up, rushing into Grandma's bedroom.

More wailing.

I buried my head in the moist pillowcase, listening to the crickets' high hum in between the moaning and consoling. I heard Mother say, "Hush, Mama. You don't have to yell so loud."

Then Mr. Alden's voice shouted from next door.

"You get 'er to shut up, or call an ambulance. We're tryin' to get some sleep over here!"

Mother told me Grandma had a cerebral hemorrhage. I remembered that just two days before I'd been telling Grandma about being invited to a hayride by a boy named Jack Nirenstein. I was hoping Mother would let me go.

"Nirenstein," said Grandma, "That's a Jew name."

I didn't like that Grandma had said his name that way.

And now she was in the hospital.

Mother said if I needed something, I should ask our tenant, Mrs. Henderson, an old lady who was home all day.

I knew I'd never ask her for anything.

"And, Shug, you be sure to call me every day as soon as you get home." she added.

~

It seemed like such a long time before I got to see Grandma, but finally one Saturday morning Aunt Gladys came by in her little coupe. Mother and I jammed ourselves in the front seat.

Aunt Gladys started dramatically telling us a story about a woman at her office who would *never, ever* use anything but a pencil stub to write with, and all three of us were laughing so hard that tears rolled down our faces. That ride was the best kind of family happiness there could ever be.

Soon we were way out in the country, parking on a gravel drive by a white-columned plantation house converted into a rest home. We entered a big, bright room with high ceilings, tall windows, and rows of beds with old people in cotton gowns and rumpled hair. I looked for Grandma and finally saw her in the middle of a row, propped up in a plain iron bed.

"Mama, here's Charlotte," said Aunt Gladys pushing me up close. "We've brought Charlotte with us today." Grandma's beady eyes were sunk in her head, her gaunt cheeks so hollow she looked close to being a Halloween skeleton. She looked right past me with no sign of recognition. Her thick curved, yellow fingernails had dirty gunk underneath.

I didn't even say, *'Grandma.'*

I guess that's what it's like to be dumbstruck. I looked past her hollow blank face to the leafy maples and tall pines outside the long window, noticing the blue sky.

~

I know I should have said something, or I could have touched her, or taken her hand, or all the things I've learned to do now at someone's bedside. I would feel better about myself today, if I had done just a little something then, but I didn't know how.

~

"Can I go outside now?" I asked.

"Stay near the car," said Mother.

Outside in the autumn sun, I picked up a rock on the gravel pathway and aimed it at the trunk of a big oak. I wished I could've cared more, but I didn't. It made me feel bad to have that dull absence of feeling.

I hit the trunk dead-on.

~

Grandma stayed in the rest home until October 4, 1950. I was in Mrs. Gray's reading class when a teacher came to tell me my grandmother had passed away. She said I was to go home. I walked to my locker in a daze to get my sweater. I didn't know what to do. I didn't know what to feel. There was no one to talk to, and I had that long walk home.

It felt so odd to leave school. I was never absent. I tucked my books under my arm and found a good-sized rock to kick all the way home.

I didn't love her. Still, she was a part of the only life I'd ever known. Soggy sweet-gum leaves lay in the gutters, turning brown from the early October rain. Waiting for a car to pass at the corner, I poised to kick the rock all the way across the street in one shot. The rock rattled on along the sidewalk.

"Step on a crack, break your mother's back" was ringing in my ears. Then I started carefully stepping over broken pavement, remembering that Grandma was dead. I felt bad and empty. Grandma was around me far more than Mother, making sure I didn't run in the street, get burned, or fall off the porch.

I remembered a story I heard once about Grandma rushing to grab me from the edge of the front porch when I was three. They said she'd fallen down those four steps shattering her ankle on the concrete walkway and had a silver wire put in to hold the bones back together. So she'd died with that silver wire still in her ankle, and I was the cause of it.

Kicking that rock helped. It gave me a physical target to attend to, taking away the numbing emptiness—something to discharge a growing anxiety. I never felt Grandma knew me or cared about me at all, just tolerated me, and it seemed to me I'd had to learn to take care of myself.

Lining up the rock at the edge of our walkway—the same walkway where my grandfather had put a bullet through his head. I aimed the rock to hit the base of the front steps where Grandma had fallen trying to protect me.

Home.

Rock of Ages.

I picked up the rock and nudged it down in the damp dirt of the concrete urn beside the leggy sunburned coleus.

~

The funeral parlor was lit with yellow sconces, mysterious and scary. Slowly I walked up to the open casket alone. I felt much younger than fourteen. Everybody was waiting to see if I was going to scream or something, but I was more curious than anything else. I noticed how long Grandma's sharp thin nose was, sticking up in profile. She looked waxy, yet peaceful, with rouge on her cheeks, wearing a new light-purple dress.

Aunt Gladys and Mother had picked out that crepe dress the day before the funeral, arguing and laughing over the color and the cost. I was grateful to be included in such a delicate moment.

"It's called mauve," said Aunt Gladys.

"Mauve?" said Mother.

Then we all laughed again. That scene, too, was like being in a real happy family, even if we were all laughing in the basement of a funeral home.

In the family receiving room, Mother seemed happy to greet old relatives and didn't shed a tear. She was wearing a navy blue hat with a short stiff veil which she kept blowing at from time to time with her bottom lip, and sometimes she pushed at it when it started tickling her nose. I was by her side being introduced to lots of old people—relatives I'd met earlier at Aunt Alice's funeral but still didn't remember, or ever think of them as *relative* to my life.

We sat with the family again, as we'd done at Aunt Alice's funeral, in the same alcove behind huge white columns, listening to a preacher read from the Bible about how Grandma was in a better place. Aunt Gladys dabbed at her eyes, her hips bulging over the edge of a small curved chair with a maroon plush seat.

There were no children my age. Cousin Sonny didn't count since I preferred to avoid him at all costs. Even at the funeral I still resented any attention Mother paid to Sonny. He was eighteen now, and huge, into Charles Atlas bodybuilding. He bragged that he could tear the Atlanta phone book in half.

Funerals can sure bring out old feelings and jealousies.

The minister read the same passage from Proverbs that he'd read at Aunt Alice's funeral, something about her *worth being far greater than rubies.*

I doubted that.

~

Back home after school Grandma's rocker looked even more empty. All during the time Grandma was in the rest home I stayed back in my own bedroom, but now I moped alone in her bedroom, sitting at her vanity dresser, mindlessly opening drawers. The lingering smell of her face powder was there, along with one of her old hatpins stuck in a crack. I saw a jar of *Arrid*, some old rouge tins, and half a row of Mother's bobby pins on a cardboard holder.

I folded in the side mirrors, leaning in, squinting to see my distant image, wondering what I might merge into—perhaps a future self. But all I saw were lots of *me's* looking back with a dishwater-blond ponytail tied with a rubber band.

It was such an empty-feeling room now. I fiddled with the worn-out red rubber atomizer, unscrewed the top, taking a sniff of lavender toilet water. I remembered Grandma sitting at this vanity getting all dressed up, and I guess it was the smell that triggered it. I suddenly remembered that once I saw her putting a book back up on top of the chifforobe.

'And don't you be gittin' this!' she'd said.

I dragged her vanity bench over and stood on it, reaching behind the curved ledge and fished out a paperback, blew off the dust, and read the title: *God's Little Acre* by Erskine Caldwell. It didn't sound very inviting with God in the title, but since it was forbidden, and I was looking to placate myself, I lay down on her bed and started reading about this family in Augusta with a girl named Darling Jill who liked rolling around naked on a bed and being spanked with a hairbrush. I wondered what they were doing that was so exciting.

Then I wondered if Grandma was up in Heaven looking down on me reading her ol' book. Even so, I figured she couldn't do anything about it now. The part about using a dowsing stick to find gold was the most interesting to me, but *God's Little Acre* didn't impress me at all, as none of the people in the book were like anyone *I'd* ever want to grow up to be.

∼

I did have the piano and some records.

Music helped.

I sauntered into the dark living room and consoled myself playing Artie Shaw's "Summit Ridge Drive" over and over on an old used record player that sometimes shorted out.

I listened to scratchy old 78-rpm recordings like "Skylark" which Aunt Clara had recently unloaded 'for Charlotte's pleasure,' feeling sorry for me. Mother's tastes were at either end of the musical spectrum, Schubert and Spike Jones.

But even music couldn't hold me together for long. The reality that I would always be alone choked me like a fishbone. I hardly spoke, and when I did, it was to complain or argue. To stay sullen and silent was to keep from screaming. If I didn't hold myself together, who would?

∼

Chapter 12

A Discovery and the Dawning Reality

AFTER GRANDMA'S DEATH Mother was on the phone wrangling with Aunt Gladys over how to divide up Grandma's house—the one they'd grown up in.

Mother said, "Shug, we have to move all our things over to the other side. Mother has to rent this side and pay Gladys, so I can own this house out right."

I didn't even care one way or the other and barely remember anything except that one Saturday, she got Moses, the yardman, to pry open the heavy sliding doors and push all the furniture across, including the upright piano, Grandma's vanity, the tier table, the divan, and the double bed from the backporch bedroom.

The first memory I have of the *other side*, was this one particularly hot day. The tiny black electric fan was whirring slowly, blowing a little comforting hot air over my suntanned body in a halter top and cotton twill shorts.

What to do?

There were no books I was interested in. I was tired of my phonograph records. I had no money to buy anything new. Everything was irritating. I flung myself down on the divan, feeling the stiff upholstery bristles against my bare legs.

I liked the living room on this side because of the French doors that opened onto the porch. Mother and I had installed new white metal venetian blinds that rattled and banged every time we came in and out of the house. Mother had done the best she could, trying to arrange things that didn't fit this smaller space, like shoving my pedestal desk in next to the big piano.

I moved to the piano stool and played "Stardust," which I'd actually learned because it was Mother's favorite. Then I picked out the first few bars of Tara's theme from *Gone with the Wind*. I knew it would make Mother smile when she came home.

I'd also been trying to learn the one-page sheet music sample of *The Warsaw Concerto* by Richard Addinsell. It was from a movie I saw—so dramatically expressive, yet sad—all the things I was feeling on that hot muggy day. Picking out a song was so frustrating, though, and I didn't have much tolerance for reading music. Still, I wanted to make Mother smile, and I needed to feel proud of something I'd accomplished.

I sauntered into the bedroom which had a big floor heater in front of a dark mantle with fat pillars. The hazy mirror over the mantle was so yellow I never even bothered to look in it. There was an ugly vent pipe attached from the heater through to the chimney of yet another cemented-over fireplace.

The old double bed was now in an alcove between two angled windows to bring in a breeze. Above the bed near the ceiling was a beautiful beveled glass window. Grandma's vanity and a single bed for Mother were squeezed in on the opposite wall.

I still loved the vanity dresser and matching vanity bench.

So romantic and mysterious!

I folded in the side mirrors, positioning them so I could see my reflection again and again, like pictures of the cow on the can of Pet evaporated milk. I peered in again, to detect some new me, but the images got smaller and smaller, blurring me into infinity—like my unknown future.

I was always hungry, so on that restless afternoon I went into the kitchen to make a sandwich. A big yellowy piece of wallpaper hung down about a foot from the ceiling. The floor was covered with a patterned piece of orange, black, and white linoleum crumbling at the edges.

The little Magic Chef gas stove Grandma once cooked my oatmeal on was moved to this kitchen. A rolling metal cart sat next to the stove with pots and pans and an assortment of boiler lids, and Mother's one big luxury, a pressure cooker. She used it a lot since she had to do all the cooking. I kept expecting it to blow up and spatter turnip greens all over the ceiling.

Against the back wall stood a tall, flimsy white metal cabinet containing odds and ends of nice things: a fancy glass plate or two, a gold-and-blue Chinese tea pot with a chipped spout, some sherbet glasses with a fascinating iridescent swirl—more of Aunt Clara's castoffs.

The cabinet was so tall and lightweight, you had to hold the edge of it when you opened the door, or you'd pull the whole thing over on the floor before the metal clasp released. But it didn't matter since we never used the things in that cabinet, anyway.

No one ever ate in here but us.

The same old white painted table with fold-down sides was in the middle of the kitchen under a light that actually had a globe around it and a long string. We had our same two kitchen chairs, no longer situated at the corners, but opposite each other now. The old black trunk and the ironing board were in the corner by a big window.

I took out a jar of *Miracle Whip* to make yet another banana sandwich. I got two slices of white bread from the breadbox we kept on top of the refrigerator and made my sandwich at the same kitchen table.

Then I took it to the narrow day bed on the enclosed backporch next to the kitchen. The window sill and the bed were at the same level, so I placed my face near the screen to catch any breeze. This was my summer hangout where I could be happy for a while just hearing the birds, seeing a bit of blue sky or feeling the cool rain, and noticing the shrubbery when it was in bloom. Still having nothing to do, I went back in the kitchen and opened up the old black family trunk with moth-eaten leather straps and rummaged around. That's when I discovered my grandfather's suicide note.

> *Dear Gladys,*
> *Please take care of Totsy and Mama.*
> *I just can't go on.*
> *Love, Papa*

I just sat there on the cold linoleum floor and stared at that note written on a scrap of ordinary tablet paper—the kind with those light blue lines—looking at the handwriting in pencil.

A suicide? Mother's father?

No one had ever told me. It was like holding something so mysterious, and yet so real, right in your hand—a piece of history—a link to your past, but one you'd never understand.

I wanted to ask Mother about it, but I was so scared. I worried she might scream over being reminded of it, or that her green eyes would narrow and she'd just clam up, and I would've hurt her beyond measure. I would never want that.

That night I couldn't come right out and say it. I was acting funny, so much so, that Mother said, "What *is it* Shug?" So then I sheepishly showed her the note.

Lo and behold, she just dismissed it, as if I'd uncovered another one of her old school books.

"Papa was upset over Mama bein' in the hospital," she said.

I was so relieved that Mother didn't break down and cry and fall apart instead of acting more or less nonchalant about my discovery of the suicide note.

Rummaging in that same trunk, I'd also found a divorce decree between Mother and a man named Walter Gray, so I asked about that, as well.

She dismissed that, too, "Oh, that was when I was *much younger.*"

~

I swear, the aftermath of Grandma dying, and us moving into the other side of the house, and then discovering the suicide note, was as if I'd awakened to find myself living in a bad movie, maybe a surreal movie.

You'd see the three of us, Mother, Grandma, and me, cast as aimless survivors: Winkin,' Blinkin,' and Nod—lost souls—bobbing around in a giant chipped teacup in a sea of flotsam and jetsam. Chunks of the aftermath of the burning of Atlanta would be floating around us. Charred pieces of Grandma's burned-to-the-ground house in 1917 would be swirling in red muddy water from the Boulevard fire; maybe we'd even see pieces of a piano that had burned up.

Then we'd see a montage of Grandma's car wreck and my grandfather's suicide—leaving her with just enough money to keep from going under. Next we'd see Grandma standing on the porch with her hands on her bony hips, seeing me arriving as a baby, and realizing she'd have to take care of me for the rest of her life.

I'm just trying to piece together some cultural and historical factors, still trying to understand.

Did anyone *ever care* about Grandma? Or Mother, *either*, for that matter? And if you don't feel cared for, how can you expect to pass it on?

Everything in the past seemed like such a mystery. I couldn't connect any dots. It was easier to be nonchalant, squelching all feelings which might bring on hysteria.

If the peeling yellowed wallpaper could've talked, it might've told me more about those accumulations of shame, and grief, and hardship, that hung like unvoiced consonants.

It's no wonder I was a careless, care-*less* person, but *still* I wanted so much to improve myself and somehow earn the right to be loved.

Yes, that was the predicament. How could I ever pass on something I'd never really felt, like tenderness or compassion?

Like a Polaroid film developing, the *shadows* of my life began to emerge, giving my life definition. This was the dawning reality of my life. I saw it all: the dust, the cracks, the shambles, how poor we were, how lacking in birthright or breeding. I calculated my odds at ever being anything like those images in the movies.

How could I ever really care about anything, except glory?

Still, I did have a dream, even if it was as undefined as just wanting to be *somebody*, to make something of myself. Even on my hopeless days, when I thought nothing *would* ever come of my life, I'd be reminded by something on the radio that this was America, the land of opportunity, where things *could* happen any day, like being "Queen for a Day," or being the lucky winner of a call-in radio program and getting free tickets as a prize.

I thought, if I just had a chance, like winning a one-way ticket to New York or Hollywood, maybe *I'd* be on the silver screen and my photo would be on the cover of a magazine, or on someone else's bedroom wall.

And a dream is a hope for the future—that one day, soon . . .

~

Chapter 13

"Don't Call Us, We'll Call You!"

THE 1950s WERE JUST BEGINNING — and *so was I*, on the cusp of adolescence. For my new Easter outfit, Mother bought me a garter belt and stockings. We picked out a navy blue belted wool jacket and low-heeled white sling-backs.

(Me, Sandra Brown, Frances Witherspoon, Kay Tallant)

On Easter morning Mother gathered my Sunday School friends in the backyard, Sandra, Frances, and Kay, and posed us holding up our skirts, looking at our first heels and stockings.

I was now shaving my legs and trying to remember to freshen up Pixie Pink lipstick.

~

And then tennis came along and things began to improve.

I couldn't believe Mother could play tennis. She bought me a MacGregor tennis racquet on sale. The next night after supper Mother said, "Guess what, Shug? I've borrowed a racquet and I'm gonna show you how to play."

Mother was just beaming that late afternoon like she'd been waiting her whole life for me to grow up so she could have a playmate. We crossed Holderness Street, the sun slanting through the tall pin oak trees, then walked up the steep hill of Greenwich Street going north, which was still cobblestoned.

Mother must've had a lot of good memories of Dargan Park as a teenager in the 20s. It would have been on her way to Lee Street School. The small park was tucked deep in the contoured valley of the next city block with double-seated swings for "courting" near the tennis court. But forty years later the park was barely kept up.

So that early evening, we walked down the other half of the steep cobblestone street into the park and began to hit a ball back and forth over an unlined clay court with a sagging net.

After those few sessions I practiced daily by hitting the tennis ball off the back of our clapboard house and then catching it on the bounce in the grass with my racquet. I did this over and over with nothing else to do. Hitting a ball off the house was easier than reading music. I liked mastering a skill that was within my range of ability. And it paid off, too. The girls' P. E. coach, Miss Happy Dowis, paired me up with Patsy Hicks to play doubles matches against other high schools once a week. We started out slowly, getting used to each other and then steadily improved, actually winning a few matches.

~

My girl friend Sandra Brown and I both played volleyball after school and walked home together. She live three blocks away on Sells Ave. She was taller than I, rawboned, sinewy like an Amazon, with a beautiful complexion, light brown hair, naturally red cheeks, blue eyes, and a pointed nose.

One day when I was turning into our short walkway, Sandra said, "Don't you just hate to go home alone?" She had an older sister and a younger brother and parents that worked.

"Nyah, I'm used to it," I said.

What else could I say? To say otherwise would be to betray all Mother's efforts to do the best she could to raise me, or to admit that I wasn't as happy and as popular as I appeared to be. When you're stuck with something, you just make the best of it. And that's when I turned—not to God—but to *chocolate*.

~

I had spending money that day and had bought a Hershey bar with almonds at Setzer's Drug Store. I dropped my books on the divan and went in the chilly, dark bedroom and yanked on the string to the overhead bare bulb illuminating the clutter.

I turned on the big gas heater. The heated metal began pinging—even the smell of burning dust was comforting. Huddled in my coat, I warmed my hands. My toes were cold inside bobby socks and suede loafers with the heel cut off, a new fad. Last year the fad was wearing a pair of moccasins, or Capezio ballet shoes with a fat rolled-down sock.

I began the ritual of unwrapping the Hershey bar and placing it in its paper wrapper on top of the heater vents. I knew just how long to wait until the Hershey bar had melted to the perfect softness. I carefully picked up the paper wrapper and slowly licked off the smooth warm chocolate, scooping up each crunchy toasted almond with my tongue, even licking the wrapper clean, like a cat. Every bar had seven almonds in it.

Those were my moments of pleasure.

The bedroom on this side had a tiny closet. It was good to have a place for my blouses, skirts, and sweaters. Mother still picked up after me, but I was much better now that I had metal skirt hangers and a closet to hang them in.

The tiny bathroom on this side had absolutely no room to turn around in. The floor was bare and cold in winter as there wasn't space for a heater. I had to sit at an angle on the toilet so my knees didn't jam into the water pipes from the bathtub—a tub so short I couldn't even stretch out.

To wash my hair, I stood at an angle because the toilet was right by the stationary wash stand. Lord, it was so hard to wash your hair with one hot and one cold faucet pouring down on your scalp. Over the toilet was a window with the ledge right at my head, so that I banged into it every time I sat on it.

On that bathroom window ledge, Mother began her unforgettable accumulation of empty containers. It started with an empty heart-shaped Blue Waltz perfume bottle that came from the dime store and an Evening in Paris bottle. Then there was an empty *Arrid* deodorant jar and a few old Tangee lip rouge tins. Tangee was a clear orangish color 30s lip rouge. Now and then she added more lipstick tubes used down to the metal rim. Mother's reasoning was that if you ever needed to, you could always dig out a little lipstick with your finger.

At first these were all spaced out and lined up on the sill, as a bathroom decoration, but then she started adding more empty containers, like tiny lipstick samples that broke off on your lips as soon as you tried to put the lipstick on. Moist bathroom dust collected over all of it.

I lived in mortal fear that someone would ask to use the bathroom, and then they'd have to walk through the messy bedroom to get to a toilet they couldn't sit straight on, and then what would they see? The cosmetic dump site.

I had the old double bed all to myself, enjoying breezes from the two double-hung windows angled to catch the breeze. On Saturday mornings I loved to just loll around on the bed, basking in that dreamy space between longing and fulfillment, watching dust particles float in a ray of sunlight, holding my hand out to catch the rainbow streaming down through the beveled glass window high over the bed just under the molding.

That was a special time, those Saturday mornings, when I could sleep late and be free of my classes, free of the worry of growing up and making good grades. I wanted to hold that rainbow in my hand and find that pot of gold at the end of it, the one that would be shaped into a gold Oscar. *If only it could stay this way and then magically I'd wake up and find out I was a star.*

I still missed Robert.

I made up a comforting daydream, which I began to call upon over and over. It went like this: Robert and I are part of a group on a cruise ship in the Pacific and have been shipwrecked. Thrashing around in the water, we finally manage to swim ashore. We drag ourselves out of the shallow water with exhaustion and collapse face-down in the warm sand. There we are, just the two of us, lying blissfully on a deserted island together. We slowly open our eyes and bask in each other's face as the waves softly splash over our feet in the warm sun.

~

Mother slept in a single bed against the other wall. It hung out over the doorway to the kitchen. Since Mother and I no longer slept together, we bumped into each other like strangers in a crowd.

I still listened to Mother's entertaining stories about Rita, in claims, who was pregnant; Doris, the switchboard operator, back from her vacation to Daytona Beach; speculations of where Roy Jr., the boss's son, was going to college; or what Mildred, in bookkeeping, had said about the new movie with Olivia de Havilland.

Mother would add, "I want to see it when it comes to the Gordon."

By then, I would have found an excuse not to go with her.

She hid her disappointment.

I hid my shame.

I remember the Saturday Mother and I ran into an office friend on Peachtree Street.

"This is my *daw-duh, Shah-lut,* she's *foat-teen* now," she said smiling.

I cringed at her deep Southern drawl, and felt equally ashamed for feeling that way, because I saw Mother's smile, being so proud of me. By now I wasn't even excited to go downtown on the trolley with Mother to the S & W Cafeteria, which had always been a favorite place for us to eat, sitting at tables around a blue-green tiled fish pool.

I had an awareness of being disdainful, but I didn't care. I never gave her credit for anything. I only now realize how Mother was helping me all along. She gave me the money to buy a little plastic ukelele and my first tennis racquet.

~

By the end of ninth grade Patsy and I played in the city tennis tournament and won our first real match. Then we won the next one. I couldn't believe this was happening to me. Then we were in the finals. The drama of it all was intoxicating.

We were *ninth graders* playing juniors and seniors. Classmates, and even teachers, asked us about our tennis results the next day at school. I belonged to something larger than my own meager life, and with a partner, too. I could never have done it alone.

Mother got off work to watch us play in the finals.

We won!

Patsy and I each received a silver engraved tennis cup.

"My goodness, Shug!" said Mother smiling so beautifully.

~

The thing is, the more we won, the more I needed to have all the recognition I could muster and no disgrace. I was so conscious of my appearance. Now that I'd begun my periods, I worried about literally sweating blood on my white tennis shorts.

I always wanted the right look—hard to do when older girls started a new fad every month. Someone said Jean B. ironed her bras to a point, so I tried stuffing toilet paper in the tips of my Whirlpool bra because I didn't quite fill out the pointed cup.

THE HORN SISTERS

I will always remember that afternoon our ninth-grade chorus was riding back on a bumpy yellow school bus, from a concert our music teacher had arranged at her alma mater,

G.S.C.W. (Georgia State College for Women) in Milledgeville, Georgia.

I was sitting next to Sandra. We'd just learned a song on the radio, sung by a girls' duo called The Bell Sisters. The song had a harmony that we'd memorized perfectly. I nudged Sandra and whispered, "Let's sing 'June Night.'"

As we finished, everyone applauded. The sound of those cheering classmates stayed in my ear.

"We're as good as The Bell Sisters," I whispered to Sandra.

All the rest of the way back home, I stared out the school bus window watching tall, spindly loblolly pines pass by, and began daydreaming about forming us into a singing duo, imagining Sandra and me as stars wearing long fur coats, dangling rhinestone earrings, and big smiles, making records. I could see our names in lights.

I wanted to have something that could take me away from what it felt like to come home every single day to an empty, desolate house. The song on the other side of the record was "Bermuda," but we needed the sheet music and accompaniment.

That night at supper I couldn't wait to tell Mother all about our bus trip adventure. She was pouring a can of Niblets corn into a dented aluminum boiler to heat for supper. I was straddling the kitchen chair, tapping my loafers on the linoleum rug, its cracked edges exposing grit particles stuck there from sweeping. The overhead globe light cast a yellow haze over the dingy kitchen.

I started naming the songs we sang, getting her interested in songs she liked, before I asked for money for sheet music to a song she'd never heard of.

As soon as I named "Smoke Gets In Your Eyes," she started singing, *"They asked me how I knew . . ."*

I continued on, "And then we sang "Night and Day.'"

"Night and day, you are the one . . .," she sang out quickly, like Name That Tune.

Then I finally said, "Guess what, Mother, when we were riding back on the school bus, Sandra and I sang 'June Night,' and the kids clapped, and some even said we were great, that Sandra and I oughta' go on the stage, or TV, or something."

"Really, Shug?" she said wiping her wet, oily brow with the worn dishtowel.

"Mother, you should've heard us. Do you think I could buy the music to 'Bermuda,' on the other side of their record?"

"Hmm," she mused.

Her voice sounded tired after her long day at the office. She was still in her work clothes, a dark brown wool skirt and plain white nylon blouse. She dumped a helping of last night's pork chops cooked in sauerkraut onto my white plate with red circles —the plate I'd eaten off my entire life.

As ravenous as I was, I didn't like fat, so I sawed it off the thin pale pork chop, while Mother eagerly gnawed all around her pork chop bone, and then forked my fat scraps onto her plate. When she was full, she wiped the grease from her mouth and chin with the dishtowel and sighed, "I guess we could manage a piece of sheet music."

The next morning when Sandra came by for school, she dropped her books on our divan to pin up a loose curler from underneath the pink and yellow chiffon scarf she'd tied over her rolled-up hair. It was a fad now to come to school with your hair still in curlers and then comb it out in the girls' bathroom. Sandra got that from her older sister, Shirley.

"Guess what?" I said, "Mother gave me the money to get the music for 'Bermuda.'"

"Gosh, really?" said Sandra looking in the mirror. "How do you like this lipstick? It's Shirley's. I put it on after she left."

She turned and showed me her lips.

"I don't like it as good as Pixie Pink," I replied.

I swear, once you started wearing lipstick in high school your lips were never to be seen without it, *ever again*, like shaving your legs. It was a teenage rule. People would think you were a member of the Salvation Army, or some other weird religious group, if you didn't.

"Yeah," said Sandra, "I think I like Pixie Pink better, too."

The next Saturday, Sandra and I set out for downtown, giddy

with excitement as we dropped in our bus tokens. After we bought the sheet music we headed over to listen to records at Rich's new sound booths. We crossed Forsyth Street, laughing and walking through the bustling Saturday-morning crowd, and took the escalator to the second floor of the new annex to their record department. We were immediately met by a sober floorwalker in a navy-blue suit who shot us a scowling look. Darting behind a large round post, we burst out in laughter.

"Boy, that guy makes me sick!" said Sandra. "Who does he think he is, anyway, J. Edgar Hoover?" That made me laugh even more. She jerked my sweater, pulling me toward the record counter.

"C'mon, let's play 'Cold, Cold Heart.'"

We asked the clerk if we could listen to the record and then took it inside the listening booth which had a window on the door.

"Let *me* put the record on," I said, afraid Sandra might scratch it with the needle. Sliding the little 45-rpm record out of its brown paper cover, I placed it over the wide spindle and gently put the needle down. Sandra was busy reading the graffiti scrawled on the white soundproof panels.

"Kilroy was here!" she read. "Boy, that guy gets around."

She popped a huge bubble, then pulled the sticky remains off her chin.

"I just love Tony Bennett, don't you?" she said. "Don't you just love him?"

We never liked the same people. I thought Tony Bennett's voice sounded like he had an adenoid problem. She was so crazy about Alan Ladd, too, and I thought he was boring with that tight little voice stuck in his throat, and I'd heard he was so short they had to stand him on an orange crate to film him kissing a girl.

I liked Nat King Cole, Jo Stafford, Doris Day, and Patti Page.

We finished listening, then handed the record back at the counter and headed out.

Sandra grinned, "Watch this, I'm gonna pop a bubble right in front of ol' J. Edgar's face."

As we whisked past the taut floorwalker, I deliberately flashed a nice smile, while Sandra blew the bubble, timing it perfectly, and POP! We dared to look back and saw him crack a tight smile.

"Well, of all the nerve—who does he think he is, anyway, Bob Hope?" she said, unsticking a thin pink film from her nose.

What I loved about Sandra was her daring, which *did* get her into trouble sometimes. I just loved the way she said things with such a happy-go-lucky attitude. I wished I could be that way. It was no wonder she was so much fun to team up with, plus she had a better voice than I did and sang the soprano part of our duets.

We asked Sylvia, a schoolmate who was also in our Sunday School class, if she would learn the music for us and be our accompanist. When she learned it, we started practicing at her house after school. Their piano was in the dining room of their neat house. Both her parents worked.

"I think we should have a name," I said, "maybe call ourselves The Horn Sisters. You know, *Bell* Sisters? *Horn* Sisters? Get it?"

Weeks later, after practicing regularly, I was in the kitchen waiting for supper, hanging onto the door jamb, swinging back and forth all excited, waiting to tell some more big news. Mother was at the stove, scraping the bottom of the pan to keep the stew from burning. She lowered the heat.

"Mother, Sylvia's daddy came in while we were singing, and guess what? He told Sylvia at supper that we were really good!"

"Well, Shug!" She blew on the hot spoon, then tasted the gravy from the stew. "Um-m."

"And then, guess what else? He told Sylvia to ask us if we'd like to sing for the Lions' Club lunch meeting at the West End Café!"

"Well, Shug. What d'ya know!"

She poured up the steaming beef stew into a big soup bowl, and her eyes kind of drifted away, like she was remembering back to when she'd had a chance . . . once, long ago, thinking about that bandleader that had asked *her* to sing once.

Sometimes Mother would say to me, when she'd be listening to a tune on the radio, "A bandleader asked me to sing once."

"Really, Mother!" I'd always say, hoping for more.

She never followed up with a "rest of the story." Then I'd lie on the bed in a dreamlike trance, making up a Hollywood scenario, picturing my mother as some glamorous singing star, filmed in black and white. I'd be there, too, in the supper club audience.

It went like this: I'd see Mother stepping up on the bandstand, her heart beating wildly, the clarinets playing the perfect intro. The bandleader would tip his head, catching her eye for her to begin. She'd smile shyly and lean into a 30s microphone with its silver art deco grillwork and sing: *Nothin' could be finah'/Than to be in Carolina/In the morning.*

She'd look out at the audience and notice a man with a cigarette as he leaned forward on his elbow. Mother would be smiling inside. The brunette next to him would raise her penciled eyebrow in approval. I'd be clapping and smiling for my mother, being so proud of her. It would be her moment of glory.

But I knew in reality she'd probably dipped her head, too shy to ever say "Yes" and take the stand.

I hadn't realized how entwined we were, like two double helixes.

I was living out her dreams.

~

In less than two months, the fifteen-year-old Horn Sisters were booked to sing for the Lions' Club luncheon at the West End Café.

On the day of our debut, we huddled in the tiny café restroom, which smelled of disinfectant—that industrial kind that comes on a little wire that hangs over the edge of the commode.

Sandra's mother had volunteered to make us costumes out of a red piqué material with big white palm leaves printed on it. She used a strapless bathing suit pattern. Sylvia's father had even bought us little flat hand drums to use when we sang "Bermuda."

"Check this out," I said, leaning into the washstand mirror, putting on a tropical red lipstick. I handed it to Sandra, blotting my lips on a Kleenex and patting the sweat beading up on my face from the tiny, hot bathroom. Sylvia had crowded in with us to help fit together the two ends of the long jacket-zipper Sandra's mother had mistakenly bought and sewn in the back.

"Oh, Charlotte!" said Sylvia, as they both started laughing. "You've blotted the lipstick all over your face."

Oh, ye gods! I looked back in the mirror in horror and embarrassment to see my face all smeary red. I started wiping it off my face, in between fits of giggling over the jacket zippers and frayed nerves. Finally we emerged from the bathroom into the tiny hallway next to the noisy, steamy kitchen, and that's when we discovered our drums were flat.

"Oh, no! Sandra, listen to this!" I said. *Thud-thud* went the drum as I hit the sagging cover, which was made of something like parchment stapled to the rim.

Sandra sang, *Down in Ber-mud-a-a,* then beat her drum, *thud-thud,* making the same dull sound. We looked at each other and burst out into nervous hysterical laughter, which exploded into a second fit of teenage giggles. We just couldn't stop and had to cross our legs to keep from wetting our sarong-looking costumes.

A stout kitchen lady in a hairnet overheard us. "Let's put them drums in the oven for a minute."

We handed them to her, then stood barefoot in our skimpy costumes, crossing our legs, stifling our laughter over and over, as we watched the kitchen ladies in hairnets and white muslin aprons lifting lids and stirring gravy. Smells of fried chicken and apple pie hung heavy.

Finally, the pleased cook opened the oven door, grabbed a potholder and removed our taut, toasted drums, as if they were two more freshly baked hot apple pies. And it worked! We let them cool, calming ourselves for our entrance, and then stationed ourselves just behind the doorway to the meeting room, pressing our half-naked bodies to the wall, waiting for our introduction. My hands and feet were ice-cold. I noticed red splotches on

Sandra's chest and neck. Then we heard our names announced. We made our entrance in homemade sarongs and painted red toenails, carrying our hand drums, and me with a plastic ukelele, to make our singing debut in 1951.

Ungracefully, we climbed on a table and sat cross-legged, looking out upon a sea of middle-aged businessmen who waited with a kind of . . . well, the image of the cartoon character Wile E. Coyote salivating, comes to mind when I recall that scene—not all the men, mind you—but a wolf-like expectation hung in the greasy restaurant air.

Sylvia played our intro on the big carved upright piano next to the American flag in its floor holder, and we began drumming a rhythm between each phrase:

(The Horn Sisters. Me and Sandra, 1951.)

Down in Bermuda, Paradise for two.
I met my lover, There on the blue.

The Lions' den eagerly applauded as we finished. Then I strummed my plastic ukelele as we sang "Roly Poly," a corny song I'd written about an animated doodle-bug. For our final number we sang "June Night," a cappella, strolling barefoot around the dusty hardwood floor among the approving Lions. I got the strolling-through-the-crowd idea right out of a Rita Hayworth number at the supper club scene in the movie *Gilda*.

We gave no thought to the meaning of the words—they were just so much rote to us, memorized off the record.

> **Just give me a June Night,**
> **The moonlight and you-oo-oo,**
> **In your arms, with all your charms,**
> **'Neath stars above, and we'll make love . . .**

We were weaving in and out between these local businessmen who sat in ladder-back wooden chairs at tables covered with red-and-white checked oil cloth. I dared not look in anyone's eyes, but noticed glasses of iced tea, pastry crumbs from slices of apple pie, little glass salt and pepper shakers, paper napkins in a metal holder, and a glass sugar jar with a chrome top.

> **I'll hold you, enfold you,**
> **And dreams will come tru-oo-oo.**

As we squeezed through the narrow seating arrangement, chairs scraped the floor, backing up so we could pass. Eager eyes followed us, though some looked down, embarrassed. I noticed a man wearing a short-sleeve starched shirt ironed like wings; another with wire-rim glasses, his arms folded across a concave chest. A red-cheeked comedian-type with bushy eyebrows that danced up and down, thrust forward when we glided by a nearby table. I'd already been too close to teenage boys panting, and even though I kept smiling, I'm sure it signaled in me a primitive fear of male sexual energy capable of going awry.

~

We weren't spectacular in any way, shape, or form, but all I could think of then was that this was the pathway to stardom!

After that first performance I got this notion that we should audition for *Stars of Tomorrow*, a local television program showcasing amateur talent. Television was new, looking for talent. There were open auditions.

I remember us giggling nervously as we rode the city bus to the WAGA-TV studios on West Peachtree Street. I was talking about the Hollywood homes we'd have in a few years.

At the studio door, a lady holding a clipboard peered at us with dark gypsy eyes and artfully penciled eyebrows. Her black hair was pulled back tightly in a bun. We were dressed in unmatching straight brown skirts and yellow sleeveless blouses and flats.

"You here for the auditions?" She tapped the board with a pencil held between long red-lacquered fingernails.

"Yes," I said.

"So, what do you do?" she asked, poised to write.

"We're the Horn Sisters," we said, almost at the same time, eyeing each other, startled at hearing ourselves announce our professional name.

"Is that a singing group?" She arched one dramatic eyebrow. Her gold loop earrings shook.

"Yes, ma'am."

She took our names and phone numbers, then said, "Do you have your music?"

"No, ma'am."

She flashed an annoyed smirk, registering, *Oh, these amateurs, these amateurs!*

"So you're singing a cappella?" she groaned.

We turned, puzzled, and looked to each other for the answer.

"We're singing 'Bermuda.'" I said, quickly adding, "It's a song The Bell Sisters recorded." I was hoping their name would give us some credibility.

"Wait over there." She pointed a red fingernail at the metal folding chairs placed around the edge of the big studio. "Mr. Miller will hear you when your turn comes."

Taking our seats on two metal chairs in the sparsely filled room, Sandra said, "Who does she think she is, anyway, Sheena, Queen of the Jungle?"

When our turn came, we stood by their piano and Sandra hit the F key. We started off fine, but got lost right in the middle when Sylvia usually played the transition. We just stopped, looking frozen in mid-air, like zombies. Finally Sandra hit the F key again, and we finished.

We blew our audition.

Mr. Freddie Miller quickly thanked us. "Don't call us, we'll call you!" he said, shuffling us off like we were contagious or something.

"Mr. Big Shot!" Sandra sneered as we picked up our billfolds off the metal chairs. "Who does he think he is, Arthur Godfrey?"

Sandra and I never heard from Mr. Freddie Miller or *Stars of Tomorrow*.

Mother and I watched the TV program the next Sunday.

"See Mother," I said poking fun at an amateurish act, "we were better than that!"

~

Mother and I watched a lot of TV in those first years of black-and-white television. I noticed every new show and was impressed that Nat King Cole had a fifteen-minute TV show playing an easy jazz style on a white baby grand. I dreamed of having a white grand piano. Still do.

I also watched the flamboyant piano virtuoso Liberace play his entertaining and impressive TV repertoire from "Three Little Fishes" to "The Blue Danube," from "Beer Barrel Polka" to "The Minute Waltz." Each week he would laughingly introduce his brother George who placed a gothic-looking candelabra on the piano. As his program ended, I would jump up and go to the piano and try out some new piano stunt.

I could do that. That's what I'd want to do, I'd think.

Then I saw a newspaper ad: "Learn the EASY Chord Method." Lessons were taught at the Arcade downtown. I begged Mother to let me try it, but she said no. I think she might've worried about sending a teenager to the downtown Arcade. She'd already turned me down for tap lessons from the Jack Epley Studio, also taught in the Arcade.

She was probably tired of putting any more money into my musical pipe dreams, anyway. I still fooled around on the piano for comfort, and one afternoon I was playing the popular 30s chord progression in the left hand and picking out "Heart and Soul" and "Blue Moon," in the right hand. Suddenly I happened to play a phrase I liked—five notes—and then I heard words to those notes:

my - true - love - has - gone

I played it over and over. A song began. I heard the trail of a melody, then added more words:

My true love has gone, like the wind and the rain.
My heart is still aching with yesterday's pain.
The angels in Heaven looked down from above
And gave words of comfort for yesterday's love.

Then it moved into the bridge with a 6/8 doo-wop beat.

They said have patience and you'll understand
It's all in the game, the work of God's hand.

And so with my head held up high in the air,
I smiled through my tears; new love was somewhere.
And now I am happy, my heart is so light
For my yesterday's love is far out of sight.

I called it "Yesterday's Love." And hadn't I always wanted to have something decent to play whenever I was around a piano? My heart started beating madly as I realized I was making up a real song, one that was good, not like that corny "Roly Poly" ukelele song I'd made up earlier and was practically embarrassed to claim.

This song was for real, something I could pull out and play like Mother playing her "Clayton's Grand March," except that "Yesterday's Love" was all mine.

I'd written words about sadness and hope and Robert, which would turn out to be the theme of my life.

~

The next big thing in my life was turning sixteen and getting a work permit to sell shoes at Rich's Department Store on Friday nights and Saturdays in downtown Atlanta for $ .90 an hour. Our Baptist Training Union Leader, Mrs. Cleghorn, was a shoe buyer and hired six of us girls. Our treasured wages came in two-dollar bills handed to us in an envelope through the cashier's window on the sixth floor. The story was that ol' Mr. Rich wanted to track how much money was spent back at Rich's.

While we were selling shoes at Rich's, I'd noticed they were televising a brand-new live afternoon television program, *Memo for Milady,* to pitch Rich's merchandise to housewives. One afternoon after school I watched the filming. Since it was summer I watched the show from home and noticed it featured a specialty singing act right in the middle, to change the Rich's merchandise set-up.

I got up enough nerve to call the TV station and ask for an audition. I told them we worked for Rich's and had costumes and a pianist. This time we took our costumes, drums, *and* Sylvia to the audition, and we were booked.

Sylvia had been our wonderful, loyal supporter, and was a real asset; her demeanor and level-headedness had the calming effect we needed. She had also added a dramatic little *glissando* right after the introduction.

Ben Gunn was our director. There was no audience, just hot lights, a cameraman, and a technician in short-sleeved plaid shirts and crew cuts. We sat on a table, resting our drums on our bare crossed legs waiting for our cue. Our song, "Bermuda," was broadcast live from the Channel 5 WAGA studios at 2:15 in the afternoon.

That first live TV appearance wasn't notable in any way, just filler in those early days of television, but I could always say we'd appeared on TV.

~

Chapter 14

I Need a Little Magic

THE PHONE RANG ONE COLD EVENING in January 1953, and a boy from my geometry class was on the other end asking about a homework assignment. This was not *any* boy, this was Richard Allen, the senior quarterback.

"Hey, I was wonderin', could you help me with problem four on our homework?" he asked.

I could picture his cute grin, though I was not impressed that he couldn't do geometry. I was glad he couldn't see where I lived with the naked 150-watt bulb glaring over the bare wooden floors, the dusty mantle, the vent pipe attached to the gas heater.

I'd been doing my homework on the unmade bed before I answered the phone, which sat on my old desk that jutted out blocking part of the door opening.

The homework assignment was a question about bisecting an angle—hard to explain on the phone.

He said, "Uh . . .well, gee, thanks . . . uh, would you like to go out after the basketball game Friday night?"

He's asking me out!

I said, "Uh . . . yeah, I guess so."

Richard was blonde with a chipped tooth and an infectious grin, a year behind his fraternal twin, Charlie, who was at Georgia Tech. I'd known them most of my life since they went to my church. His mother was the Sunday School Superintendent.

Richard never knew *his* father, either. His mother had raised the twins and an older brother Earl, all by herself after her husband died of TB when Richard was two.

That Friday night after the game, I was scared waiting for him in the gym lobby, as he had to change out of his basketball uniform.

Why would he want to date me? I kept asking myself.

Then I saw him coming through the locker room door, wearing his blue and gray football jacket, his hair still wet from a shower. His lip was swollen from a cut during a jump ball scuffle.

"That was some game, huh?" he said.

"Yeah, we won!" was all I could manage to say.

He was so wonderfully genuine and boyishly shy, which put me at ease. We climbed in the backseat of his cousin Eugene's car, who'd been waiting for us with his steady date, Anne. Eugene drove us to Joe Cotton's, the Brown High drive-in hangout, where we ordered hamburgers and frosted oranges.

Our next dates were just afternoons of throwing his football in the long green field by John A. White golf course, running, kicking, and cavorting, like a couple of young, happy colts. He was so happy I was interested in his football skills.

He kept saying, 'Gee, Charlotte, really?' when I asked him to show me how to throw a pass.

"Now watch!" he said. "See where my fingertips are? You gotta give your signal count, then grip the edge of the laces *right away*, step back, wait for your receiver, then throw from above your shoulder and follow through. Okay. Go out."

I ran out and then I saw a beautiful brown oval spiraling toward me and I caught it, hugging it into my chest.

I was as happy as he.

I loved learning this sport he played so well.

Another afternoon he taught me to center the ball. I bent over holding the football on the ground. He was behind me and put his hand on the inside of my thigh, lightly touching it.

"Yi-ih!" I startled.

"Don't jump," he laughed. "That's so the center'll know where the quarterback's hand is. C'mon, when I say hut-four, slap it in my hands, run out ten yards, then cut left."

I did . . . and another perfect spiral hit me.

He played tennis and was as much of a performer as I. He showed me some jitterbug steps and soon we had worked up a fancy dance routine in my living room.

He was the perfect boyfriend.

After our football romps we would sit in the car in an empty part of the golf course parking lot and pet. I remember the sun slanting through the windshield of his mother's blue Plymouth— the fragrant scent of honeysuckle wafting through the car windows. He combed my hair. I put my head in his lap and he massaged my eyelids and eyebrows.

It was a long spring of enjoying the pleasure of touch, in and of itself, and not as foreplay. I didn't worry about it, either. It was just understood that we wouldn't 'go all the way.'

One afternoon we were sitting in the car, petting in the warm sun, just fondling each other's arm or face, enjoying the sensation of touch and texture. His hand slid along the inside thigh of my jeans, barely touching the double-stitched seams. My jeans were pressing tightly between my legs, and I slowly began to feel a warm, tingling spasm in my crotch . . . then a wonderful pulsation . . . a flooding . . . like sunlit water rushing in between my legs. Such an exquisite pleasure I'd never felt before. I didn't say anything. I wasn't breathing hard, just utterly relaxed and blissful.

ONWARD CHRISTIAN SOLDIERS

On Sundays I left for the Baptist church, fit to kill as they say, starting out with wriggling into a tight elastic girdle, stockings, white nylon slip, and light blue suit. It ended with me donning a white straw hat, light blue heels and white gloves in the latest 50s fashion. I forced myself to sit through the first Sunday School assembly. My only respite was a boogie-woogie touch to the hymn "No Never Alone" from irreverent Mrs. Venable, the substitute pianist.

From assembly we filed into our classroom that was decorated with pictures of Jesus and scenes from the New Testament. We perched on small chairs in a semi-circle, like nylon-kneed biddies, holding Bibles on our laps, our garter snaps poking up through our tight skirts. Our Sunday School teacher reminded us to save ourselves for the right Christian man.

After Sunday School our gaggle of girls hurried down the wide stone church steps and across the narrow street to Clyatt's Drug Store where we stood bunched in like sardines, trying not to jostle the fountain cokes we held in gloved hands.

Richard would be there with his buddies, boys dressed in white bucks, thin black ties, and narrow suede belts in the waistbands of their black pegged-pants.

I saw Mother across the drugstore crowd chatting with her Sunday School friends in The Gleaners Class. The black and white tiled floor pressed painfully through the soles of my too high, too tight shoes; I would get no sympathy from Mother for buying cheap ones from Butler's.

As I yakked away sipping my fountain coke, smiling like a movie star, I tried to think of reasons why a Hollywood producer might happen to come to this drugstore. Maybe he would be a long-lost brother of Dr. Clyatt, the pharmacist, and he would have just a few hours in town, since he was casting a new movie. He would look over at me in my jaunty white straw hat, smiling with my almost even white teeth, and see I was perfect for the part. Unrolling a parchment contract, the crowd would part as I made my way to a wrought-iron ice cream table where I would remove my white glove so I could sign my Hollywood contract.

My mind was always going off on some movie-making tangent. I tacked an old towel on the end of the clothesline pole and staged a scene of Sandra, Sylvia, and me in a reenactment of raising the flag on Iwo Jima,.

Cousin Sonny, now a senior at Oglethorpe University, had been cast in the student production of *You Can't Take It With You.* Mother and I went to see him in the little theater auditorium. Sonny was incredibly funny, much to my chagrin, and got lots of applause at his curtain call.

Afterwards, Mother kept raving over his comedic acting. I was jealous of him getting that kind of adulation. I wanted to outdo him.

Most of all, I wanted to be able to say to people, *I'm going to college.* Somebody that had a college degree *was somebody*! That's all there was to it, in my book. A diploma was something that could never be taken away.

In August just before Richard went to Florida on a football scholarship, he gave me his football jacket and said 'write me,' so that meant we were going steady. I felt good because I didn't have to worry about who would I date my senior year and I could still feel popular.

I started back to school, but when I looked at my schedule I had a sudden apprehension about everything. *Lord!* Besides college English and biology, I was scheduled for trig, social problems and Latin II.

What little confidence I had went straight out the door, so I didn't even try out for basketball or cheerleading, because it was enough to still be on the tennis team.

I *had* been thinking a lot about college though. I'd heard that the Supreme Court had changed the law, so I got to thinking I could be the first white girl to go Spelman. I could live at home and practically walk there. From my point of view, I thought Spelman was a good possibility because on my many trips to downtown Atlanta, I had regularly passed by Spelman College with its white-columned brick buildings and beautiful manicured lawns. It had a familiar appeal to me, being so close to home and all. In my imagination I figured I'd be an interesting novelty and some girl or other would probably want to be friends—no, not many, but a few.

~

Mother was warming up leftover meatloaf, easing thick, cold slices into the little black iron skillet. I was nervously twirling the salt shaker on its side because I knew what I was about to discuss. She opened up a can of green beans and dumped them in a pan to heat.

"Mrs. Cox gave me an application to fill out today to the University of Georgia," I said.

"I don't know where we'd get the money."

"I know," I sighed. "What about me going to Spelman?"

"Shug!" said Mother in disbelief. "And stop that, you're flinging salt out."

"No, I'm not. Centrifugal force keeps the salt in," I retorted, continuing to spin.

I was just sounding her out, wanting to see her reaction. I knew how she felt about colored people.

~

Thinking about Spelman and integration, I remember when a new maid, Maggie, came regularly to cook, wash clothes, iron, and empty Grandma's slop jar. I hardly ever spoke to her, but I remember this one day after she'd been with us for a while, I'd been curious about her wages which were referred to as *fifty cents and car fare.*

I was in the front walkway where I'd drawn off squares with some chalk and was playing hopscotch when I noticed Maggie coming around from the back of the house on her way home.

"Maggie," I asked, "How come you don't ever take the street car?"

"I saves the fifteen cents."

"Where do you live?"

"Off Fair Street."

"How far is it to your house?"

"Long ways."

"How long do you think?"

"Maybe 'bout three miles. I best be gittin' on."

I watched her for a long time that day, plodding down the sidewalk. I knew she'd soon cross a dividing line between the colored and white people. Maybe it was the way Maggie walked that day, her heavy ankles spread out over rundown black Oxfords, plodding that weary, joyless gait, that made me feel so sympathetic to her lot in life.

Then again, she probably felt that way about my lot in life.

Another time I asked, "Maggie, why are you called colored? There's no red or blue about you."

She got real angry that day and said, "I am a NEEgro, not a colored person, and not a NIG-ra, either!"

We were standing in the side yard that day, by the fence where tiny wild potatoes grew on a vine, and people said you shouldn't eat them because they were poison. Funny how that memory is still so clear. Maybe it was something about the word *poison*—something that will kill you. Poison in a culture that I already felt.

I remember her look of anger so well—something about being treated with human dignity, and I'd somehow crossed that line by asking why she was called *colored.*

She looked straight at me that day with her dark eyes and yellow eyeballs.

"Don't you be callin' me anything but a NEE-gro!"

Lord, I was afraid to look at her straight on after that.

And, though I felt her plight, I didn't ask her any more questions.

~

Mother forked a slice of meatloaf onto my plate, adding the beans. I poured a glass of milk and got the loaf of bread down out of the breadbox. I took two pieces. I peeled off the wide crust, then mashed the soft bread into a round dough ball and popped it into my mouth. Mother poured catsup over her meatloaf and took a big mouthful, leaning over her plate.

All during supper, I'd been postponing showing Mother my mid-semester report card, which had a D in social problems.

Now let me tell you about the social problems class that I hated more than any other in my entire five years at Brown High.

First of all, we had to read books like *Learning About Ourselves* and then give oral book reports. Second, I chose to sit on the back row in the corner because I felt so intimidated just by the class subject. Of all people I sat behind Roy Turner. He had mossy teeth with spit bubbling out of the corners every time he spoke. He'd drag his scummy finger across my desk, or touch my notebook, or let his arm dangle in the aisle by the wall, so no one would see him *but me*, and "shoot birds" with a dirty fingernail on his middle finger.

He loved to say embarrassing things, like one day before class had begun, he turned around in his desk and sang, "*Oh, my bucket's got a hole in it/ Oh, my hole's got a bucket in it,*" and I just wanted to crawl up under my desk and *die*.

Classmates would be giving book reports about some very personal things and Roy would turn around sideways and make a snide comment, so I knew I could not possibly get up and make a book report.

Our teacher Mrs. Purvis was a character right out of a movie. She had puffy white hands with tapered fingers, so dainty she couldn't squeeze out a wet washrag. She spoke in mincing mouthfuls, pursing her tiny pink lips over prominent eyeteeth, which gave her a twitchy rabbit look. Her blondish hair looked as if she had taken out the bobby pins and just left the pin-curls uncombed. Her tiny eyes with blond lashes darted around, blinking and fluttering—not on purpose—more like she was thinking too fast.

The irony of this class was that one day Mrs. Purvis wrote on the board a list entitled, "The Needs of Every Human Being." The two I remember were 'to belong' and 'novelty.'

Something deep inside me resonated that day—some deep interest I already had in human nature. I made an entry in my diary that I might major in psychology.

And I wound up with a D at mid-semester because I hadn't done any oral book reports. I had postponed telling Mother about my report card for two days, and I knew I couldn't hold out any longer.

As we sat on the sofa watching *I Love Lucy*, at a commercial I said, "We got our report cards. Ya' want me to go get it?"

"Is it good?"

"N-n-not really."

I went to the bedroom to get my report card. The worst thing about making good grades was that you had to keep it up. Boy, I hated that pressure. It was just too awful, and I was depressed as I slowly walked back into the living room, slumped onto the divan, and laid the card in Mother's lap.

When Mother saw the D, she pitched a fit!

"It's just *mid-semester*, Mother!"

Lord, she started ranting like a madwoman, got herself all worked up over it, talking about how she was going through the 'change' and 'how could I do this?'

I just sat there numb, saying nothing in defense. I'd never, ever seen Mother mad at all, and now she was a raving lunatic. At one point she stood over me with a slipper in her hand, waving it around, and I thought she was going to hit me. I moved off the divan over to the piano stool. Then she was leaning into me and spit drops hit my face as she spewed out her fury. Then she backed off and actually threw the slipper at me, but I ducked. What a scene!

I think Mother blew up over my D because she'd said to me more than once, "Don't *ever* tell anyone I didn't graduate from high school." She'd foolishly taken millinery her senior year and didn't realize she wouldn't have enough credits to graduate until it was too late. And she was seeing the same thing happen to me.

Miss Rikard, my homeroom teacher, said I needed two years of a language to get into her alma mater, Agnes Scott, but I just couldn't hack all that Latin II translation, or the trig class either. I was so afraid of making a bad grade, I dropped them both and switched to art and typing, knowing I'd lost my chance to get into a better college, or any college for that matter.

I needed a little magic.

~

Chapter 15

'49 Ford with Twin Smitties

I HAD A TERRIBLE COLD AND ACHING SINUSES the Saturday I was to take a scholarship test for the University of Georgia. Sitting at Grandma's old vanity with the fold-in mirrors, I took bobby pins out of my rolled-up hair and sneezed again. I saw swollen puffy eyes. My head was killing me. I took two aspirins and combed out dishwater blond hair, parting it on the side, arranging the peroxided bangs just so, the current fad.

Then I started feeling sick at my stomach, wondering what on earth I was doing, setting myself up for another blow to my fragile self-esteem. I wanted to crawl back in bed on my precious Saturday morning. How could I even be thinking about taking a scholarship test? I knew I wasn't that smart. Not by a long shot.

I kept thinking over and over: What does it really matter whether I take this test or not? Does anyone really care whether I go to college? No one, but me. Even if I do get a scholarship, it'll only be for tuition.

I could so easily have crawled back in bed. Mother would've understood. She wouldn't have pushed me. I wouldn't disappoint anyone, not the school counselor, or my homeroom teacher. None of my girl friends were going to college, or hardly *any* girls from my high school. I wasn't quite a dumb blonde, but I wasn't too serious about anything, except performing.

If there was ever a turning point in my life, though, it was that Saturday, because I did manage to finish getting dressed without caving in to laziness or insecurity.

What swayed me, I think, was that I figured it was better *to* take that test, than *not to* take that test. Simple as that. So we got in Mother's car and drove across town around the square in Decatur, looking for a drugstore where I bought my first nose inhaler. I remember that it didn't help at all. I was all scrunched down in the front seat worried about *anyone* seeing me in this hot-rod sounding two-door '49 Ford—the car I'd begged Mother to buy last summer with my senior year approaching.

~

I must pause here and tell you the story of Mother buying that first car.

My boyfriend Richard had been driving me to school since January. In August when he was leaving for college, I started pleading to Mother, "Please, please, can't we get a car? I'm so tired of hitching rides or walking."

Not long after that on a hot summer night in 1953, our tenants went looking for a newer car themselves and took us along to a used-car lot on Lee Street. A snappy, used-car dealer spotted Mother and showed her a black two-door '49 Ford with twin smitties.

"Jes' look at those *babies*," he said, pointing to two large, shiny chrome exhaust pipes—mufflers, which he called 'smitties' —were extending from underneath the rear bumper.

Handing Mother the keys, he lured, "Take 'er for a spin!"

Then the burly salesman, smelling of Vitalis and whiskey, pushed the front seat back for me to get in, and he sat up front with Mother.

I'd never seen Mother drive, and I was excited to see her slide under the wheel. She turned the key, gunned the engine, and I heard the low rumble of those dual mufflers.

Mother's seersucker dress was sticking to her back on that humid summer night. Maybe she was nervous—you know, like bravado, or something—because she started telling the salesman about the time she first drove her papa's car.

"One day when Papa had gone off to work on the streetcar," she said, "I just cranked up that ol' Model T and backed it right out the driveway."

The salesman slapped the dashboard, laughing as Mother drove fearlessly out of the used-car lot, past colorful flapping pennants hanging over the entrance, then around the block while our tenants waited.

After we got back home, when I found out she hadn't plunked down a deposit, I started to bawl. I'd never had my heart set on anything as much as us having a car. I cried every day like I'd been sentenced to be executed.

Mother gave in.

The used-car salesman came over the next Saturday and took Mother to get her driver's license. Two weeks later, Mother bought it for $500. She gave me some driving lessons on a deserted road, but I was afraid to drive and had no interest, so I wound up walking to school my senior year.

~

Back to that Saturday scholarship test. In the large classroom at Decatur High, I settled myself in a shiny blonde student desk, wanting to lay my stuffy head down, close my watering eyes, and just go to sleep. But I started filling out the scholarship application forms.

To the question of Mother's occupation, I wrote cashier/bookkeeper, wishing Mother had some better job, something fancy and executive sounding.

The next question was: Family Income. The increments started with $2400-3000 annual. Not knowing exactly what Mother made, I marked an X in the lowest category. Even with the $34 a month she got from my father, I was sure it was under

$3,000. Acknowledging the reality of our financial condition by marking an X in the lowest category made me sick to my stomach.

The three-hour scholarship test was both easier and harder than I expected, and I was mainly just relieved when time was called.

Soon it was the Spring of my senior year. Our annual high school variety show was coming up. Sandra and I planned some new songs and announced the news to anyone listening in the girls' bathroom. Then a rumor started that some boys had been calling our little singing duo "The *Horny* Sisters."

I didn't get what was so funny.

"It means you want to 'do it all the time,'" said Patsy one day walking home from tennis practice. She'd already told me about something called a rubber her brother carried in his wallet.

I still didn't *get* what any of that meant, but *horny* sounded slutty, and I would never want that image. I could just imagine who it was that started it—the boys who now drove hot-rods and were reported to be playing "chicken" out past the Bankhead Highway.

"We *have* to change our names!" I said to Sandra.

"Like what?" she asked.

"To the Coconettes," I said thinking of those palm leaves on our red costumes. "Let's start practicing our new songs."

Sandra's mother offered to make new costumes. Soon, I was at a fitting at the Brown's house, standing nervously as Mrs. Brown pinned up the short black satin hem using the same strapless bathing suit pattern. We laughed and kidded her about buying the right zippers this time.

Being in their house again, I was remembering that Sandra and I had known each other since second grade, burning Toll House cookies together in her kitchen, forming the Polly Pigtails Club in her basement, playing softball, high school tennis, volleyball and basketball, double-dating, touring with the church youth choir all the way to New Orleans and Miami, and getting into the only fight I ever got into—arguing over being safe, or out, on third base, punching and shoving each other in her front yard on Sells Avenue.

~

In the Spring of 1954, almost 600 people were packed into the hot Brown High auditorium—parents, grandparents, brothers, sisters and teachers. The new eighth-graders were hanging over the balcony, basking in their sub-freshman year of high school spirit, waiting to see their first student variety show.

We sang our first two numbers, "Midnight" and "Blow Out the Candle," in our new black satin costumes. Sylvia was still our dutiful accompanist.

Then for our finale, we stepped out in front of the heavy maroon curtain in black high heels and canes. The follow-spot moved along as we sang "Side by Side." We smiled and did a little dance routine we'd learned from two lessons at a dance studio in West End. The audience whistled and cheered. It was such a fitting ending song for our last appearance and the end of our singing career.

Sandra was voted runner-up most athletic. I was runner-up best all-around. I wanted Sandra to study harder and go to college like her sister. I wanted us both to get married and live next door to each other so we could go on laughing and singing together our whole lives.

~

On the night of our graduation, I wasn't even feeling sad as I sat on the stage of the city auditorium in a white evening dress among sad and excited classmates—the Brown High School Class of 1954. I was picking at a thread unraveling in the stitching of my only pair of white cotton gloves, listening to my old boyfriend, Robert, give the valedictory speech.

I still had feelings over losing him, but that night I was stewing over a bigger loss—losing the state doubles tennis championship that very morning in Macon, then having to come back as a loser for graduation.

We lost. That's all I could think about, sitting on that auspicious stage. I was such a bad loser. I tried to act like a good sport and laugh it off, or make excuses, but I was dying inside. A silver medal isn't bright when last year we'd won the gold.

For a whole year we'd been heralded as the 1953 Georgia State Doubles Tennis Champions.

Mrs. Swain, our choir director, motioned with her hand for us to rise, and one hundred and fifty seniors sang "I Believe," a new song introduced through television in 1953. Later in the program we sang "You'll Never Walk Alone" from *Carousel*—two unforgettably beautiful moments.

Then our red-faced principal waddled to the lectern, adjusted his glasses, cleared his throat, and began to read the names of the scholarship recipients. His fat jowls swayed loosely as he spoke.

He wouldn't be reading my name.

By the time I'd received notice of my freshman scholarship award, others in my class had received notices of four-year full-tuition grants to Yale, Georgia Tech, Tulane, and Vanderbilt. I viewed my scholarship award to the state party school with disdain and didn't inform anyone. Apparently no one informed our school counselor, either.

I knew Mother and Aunt Gladys were in the audience tuning up to cry as soon as they heard the processional, "March from Aida." The least I could've done was to tell my homeroom teacher I'd received an award, so I could give Mother the joy of hearing my name announced in the city auditorium as the recipient of a freshman scholarship to the state university.

But I didn't.

I couldn't even enjoy my own graduation. I would have wanted that part of my life to end on a high note, but, I swear, as soon as I lost at anything—like that tennis match—I could feel my entire life going down the drain. I would just get stuck on that dot, seething and ravenously hungry!

I'm sure I was a rotten date that night. My boyfriend Richard had come home from The University of Florida to accompany me to the dance and afterwards to make the ritual climb to the top of Stone Mountain. I was only too ready to devour cheese grits, country ham and eggs, biscuits, red eye gravy and peach cobbler at the graduation breakfast.

I wonder sometimes when people say they don't regret anything in their lives, if they really mean it, because I have lots of regrets. I regret being uncaring, selfish, and inconsiderate. I regret viewing everything that wasn't topnotch with disdain and being a bad sport. I regret all of my dismissive, haughty behavior —especially the way I ignored Mother and her feelings.

~

Mother let me send my father a graduation invitation, and I got a card back signed with that same scrawly signature. It was addressed to *me* this time, not Mother. It meant so much to me, like he actually knew I existed, just by addressing my name, *Miss Charlotte Ashurst* in his own handwriting.

I tucked the card away and daydreamed that one day I'd be so famous, he would come and meet me in my tiny backstage dressing room—for I had checked speech and drama as my major. I would've preferred art or music, or even psychology, but I had nothing to prove I had any talent, much less brains. I did have stage and TV appearances, so I figured they might accept me as a drama student.

~

In June a letter arrived: Welcome to the Drama Department. Then an envelope arrived with a brochure: Welcome to the University of Georgia Panhellenic.

I was beginning to feel like one of Grandma's radio soap-opera heroines: *"Can this little girl from a crummy house on the wrong side of town find happiness at the state university?"*

The only thing I knew about sororities was from two B-movies: *Betty Co-ed* and *Sorority Girls*. Those movies depicted a bunch of well-dressed, rich, petty, snobbish, two-faced co-eds, vying for membership and boyfriends. They dressed in expensive sweater sets, flaunting a fraternity pin stuck right on top of a cashmere covered pointed breast.

I relished every minute of those movies, in spite of their *Betty Co-ed* shallow and meaningless behavior, I wanted to be a part of it all.

I must be mad, I thought.

I didn't dare mention to Mother that I was considering sending in a rush card. She'd sigh and heave her expression, 'Hee-e-e, Me.'

Hearing her sigh would be discouragement enough.

~

All during that restless summer of 1954 I was employed in Mother's office in the stockroom, pulling mangled envelopes from a mailing machine with Jane Griggs, whose father was the claims' manager. We were both headed for college and were paid $140 a month.

"Did you get your rush information?" Jane asked.

"Uh-huh." I acknowledged guardedly.

We were also using the three-hole punch to make colored paper confetti to toss out the window for the Fourth of July parade. We planned to watch from the stockroom window, since it overlooked Peachtree Street at Five Points—a wide window with no screen or railing, just soot and pigeons on a parapet—a window you could easily jump from.

Jane said, "I'm gonna pledge Zeta. My sister Muffy is one. It's really one of the best sororities. Muffy said it's *the* best. Daddy drives us over for the games. The house is beautiful! Are you going out for rush?"

"I don't know yet."

"Well, you'll have to be sure to go to the Zeta house and say hello to Muffy."

I was pea green with envy, like Scarlett, blushing from my ignorance of such social matters. I bit off the rough edge of a fingernail, grinding the hard surface savagely and comfortably between my teeth.

I hated being reminded of this huge class gap I was hurdling myself into. I wanted never to have to think about *that part*—the class difference—a social sphere more educated, sophisticated and worldly than mine. I was fairly pretty, had made the Beta Club, and was a tennis champion, but how far would that take me?

To avoid eating lunch with Mother or Jane, I brought a book. I was so afraid of something coming up about sororities, and I just couldn't deal with it, so I stayed in the stock room alone, eating a mushy banana sandwich, looking down from that window sill which overlooked those five streets known as Five Points. It was hard enough to chew and swallow my own social-climbing diet.

I couldn't concentrate on Rima the bird-girl in *Green Mansions*, a book on the college reading list. My mind was in such a turmoil of emotions, buffeting me against the edges of deceit and guilt for my enormous desire to be in a sorority, like a poor child in rags pressing her face against a store window at Christmas.

I tried to think of something else.

I'd never really looked down at Five Points from five stories up. I remembered reading that those five bustling streets of traffic had once been no more than Indian trails that Sherman's troops had marched down them with horses pulling supply wagons on dirt roads. I was remembering my fondness for that scene with Scarlett and Rhett heading out of town. One of those intersections led out to the Decatur Road. Rhett was covering the horse's head with his coat so he wouldn't bolt as they drove through the burning of Atlanta—part of my history, too. And to think—Mother had met my father at the drugstore downstairs, right here in the heart of Atlanta.

~

It was a Saturday, and Mother was out. I propped my suntanned legs on the curved back of the divan, looking at the Panhellenic booklet. I'd begged Mother to redecorate, and she finally had the divan reupholstered in a dusty-rose brocade. The dark woodwork and mantle had been painted white and the walls wedgwood blue.

The Panhellenic booklet showed photos of elegant antebellum sorority houses—more beautiful than Tara from *Gone with the Wind*. I looked at the reply card.

How will Mother ever pay for this? Oh, never mind. I'll worry about that tomorrow! Just fill out the card!

But then I started to hate my own name.

Charlotte. So formal.

Hmm? Muffy, what a cute name! How come I can't have a cute name like that? Say, what if I change my name? No one will know me at college.

I wrestled like St. Peter with this conflict of the heart, urging me against my better nature not only to sell my Christian birth name, but also to sell my soul for a sorority. I was coming to believe that, like Peter, I would've denied Jesus in order to be well thought of, and to look good in the eyes of others.

In the meantime I'd been smoking Pall Malls. I kept my pack hidden high up on a built-in kitchen cabinet. I'd been taking drags off Richard's Chesterfields on every date. I went to the kitchen and climbed onto a chair to retrieve a cigarette. Back in the living room I lit up my Pall Mall with a long kitchen match and pondered the rush card.

As I blew out Hollywood smoke, I looked in the mirror over the white mantle, watching it waft around my head. I smiled at myself letting smoke float through my carefully parted lips, holding my hand just so.

The other part of me was fraught with thoughts of the foolishness of rubbing elbows with select girls who probably had mothers that stayed home and gave tea parties or drank highballs and shopped at Muse's or Regenstein's department stores.

I couldn't keep myself from wanting it. Still, I was afraid to send in the rush card. I knew I was setting myself up for a huge disappointment and probably humiliation.

As I was pacing like Bette Davis, nervously blowing smoke out the living room window screen, I remembered our senior trip when we were all smoking like crazy, crowded into one room at the Seaside Motel on Daytona Beach. Girls would fall down laughing on the twin beds when someone started coughing and choking and practically passing out. Sandra and I started using a code word, calling cigarettes *chips,* as in potato chips.

On the daily travel bus, Sandra would say, "Are y'all gonna have some *chips* tonight?" Meaning: 'Are you going to smoke cigarettes back in the motel room?'

And we'd laugh hysterically, and I'd say, "Yes-s! We're gonna have two bags of *chips!*"

I ground out my ashes on the window screen. I was sure my smoking went undetected. Suddenly a name popped in my head. What about *Chips*? That's cute. *Chips Ashurst.* Yes! That's much better than my real name, Charlotte. I had a raging impulse to write *Chips* on the rush card.

And I did.

But when I said it out loud, *Chips Ashurst,* the alliteration was terrible. *Dang!* I'd written it in ball point pen. I ran to the kitchen and found the Clorox and bleached out the *s*.

The card looked messy, but I mailed it off.

Three weeks later I received a letter in the mail to *Chip Ashurst*. I'd completely forgotten about changing my name on the rush card. The next day two more *Dear Chip* letters arrived. With each letter I got out my Panhellenic brochure and matched up photos of the beautiful sorority houses with those wonderful girls who were writing to *Chip*.

Thank goodness they couldn't see where I lived in this three-room dump. Never mind that for now, I thought, reveling in all those personal invitations.

One letter writer wrote, "What a cute name!"

Exactly what I wanted to hear.

Twelve letters arrived. I spread them out on the daybed where I was sprawled by the long window and began to compare handwriting, use of the English language, and kinds of stationary. I memorized the three Greek letters in each sorority's name. I noted each letter-writer's name with her sorority, so I could be sure to meet her.

Rolling over on my back I held a sheet of lavender-colored stationery above my head and sighed.

Oh, yes, yes, yes! I want to visit all of you—in all of your beautiful sorority houses. I want to join all of your sororities.

~

SEPTEMBER 19, 1954

If ever there was a miracle day in my life, this was it. We were loading the car for college.

Hallelujah!

All Sunday morning Mother and I had packed the little black Ford with clothes, shoeboxes, a red gooseneck lamp, sheets, towels, blue-ribbed Bates twin bedspreads, and my tennis racquet. I finally loaded the last item, my large hatbox, cramming it on top of everything else in the back seat.

"Shug, Mother won't be able to see out the back window," said Mother as we stood on the sidewalk mopping perspiration from our faces. She was wearing a two-piece navy dress with a small white flower print. Her hair was damp around her neck.

I had bought three dresses at Regenstein's on sale for $10 each. I was wearing my favorite, a lightweight herringbone rayon-cotton flared dress trimmed in tiny red piping with a Chinese collar, and round red buttons all the way down the front. I had on red leather pumps with a low square heel.

Red and black—the colors of the University of Georgia.

~

It was a long two-lane eighty mile drive to Athens that Sunday. We passed through Stone Mountain, Snellville, Loganville, and Monroe. As Mother pulled into the Myers Hall parking lot, I wished we weren't arriving in a car that sounded so trashy. I didn't even want Mother to help me bring in my clothes, but I didn't want to hurt her feelings.

As I met other freshman girls, I introduced myself as Chip Ashurst, trying to act blasé.

I don't want to be Charlotte anymore. I want to be a new person. But already I was feeling deceitful and guilty, again. Defensively, I said to Mother, "You saw all those 'Dear Chip' letters I got."

I didn't even have to look at Mother's expression to know she was thinking I'd get what was coming to me, because I'd changed my Christian name which she'd given me at birth. I could read that from one twitch of her mouth. But in fact, she just stood there smiling blankly in an awkward way, waiting for me to lead the way—onward and upward—to find my third-floor room.

My new roommate, Nancy, and her mother and father were busy unloading two trunks. I could see they had more money and better taste than I. After the last load Mother stood hesitantly at my dorm room door, clutching her purse. I'd put my red gooseneck lamp on the metal desk and it was *my* room now. I didn't encourage her to stay and help me get settled.

Back downstairs we got in the car. Mother drove across the hot Myers Hall parking lot and stopped under the shade of a big oak to say our goodbyes. Her chin quivered as she turned off the engine. Suddenly, after being all caught up in my own grandiose plans, I felt overwhelmed with Mother's feelings. A lump came in my throat because I knew Mother would be all alone now. I was leaving her. I sensed it would be forever.

As we sat together in that car I hated, but which had brought me to the university, my hopes and dreams were bursting inside like sparklers. Hot tears stung, then welled up in my eyes, and an awful ache came in the roof of my mouth.

I didn't want to *lose it* and cry, not now.

I knew how much I meant to her—how much she quietly bragged about me. I sensed what a moment in time this represented. This was the death of the little twosome we'd been for eighteen years—not really mother and daughter—more like jolly companions and fellow entertainers in a kind of comic soap opera journey.

Up until today.

Today we would part. Mother would drive the long way home, all by herself. I wouldn't be there when she got home from work on Monday to hear the stories of the girls in the office. I wouldn't be there to eat supper at the kitchen table. I wouldn't be there to see the wallpaper hanging down from the ceiling, or stare at that torn linoleum floor, or grab a piece of bread from the metal breadbox with the red wheat decal. I wouldn't have to see the greasy Magic Chef gas stove with long porcelain knobs, or the pitted kitchen sink that stood on metal poles with the trash can underneath, or the ironing board with the scorched cover hovering in the corner by the black family trunk with the worn leather straps, that held the family Bible with birth names written in ink.

We sat silently and awkwardly with tears flowing down our cheeks. Then we looked at each other and laughed at ourselves for crying. Mother dabbed at her eyes with a Kleenex and blew her nose. I was anxious to get back to my new room and new friends.

"Be sweet, Shug. Write me."

"I will."

"Be a good girl."

"I will."

Tears well up in my eyes—even now—as I write about those lingering moments of saying goodbye in the dorm parking lot.

I felt that excruciating pain of separation and leaving home. I didn't know what was ahead, but I knew I was never going back.

That was the saddest day of my life, and it was also the happiest, and was, coincidentally, my eighteenth birthday.

I got out of the car. Her chin quivered again as she cranked up the engine and slowly drove out of the parking lot, and onto the side street, passing me once again. Swallowing back tears, I waved, hoping she'd stopped crying by now. She managed a quick wave back and then gunned it a little as she pulled out into the Sunday traffic. I watched until the car was out of sight on Lumpkin Street, listening to the distant low rumbling of those twin mufflers.

Finally . . . they too . . . faded away.

~

Chapter 16

The Drama of a Drama Major

EVEN THOUGH IT WAS WONDERFUL to be in college, I was wary when it came to disclosing too much about myself. I met girls on my floor from towns in Georgia I'd never heard of: Brooklet, Dewey Rose, Metter, Willacoochee, and Cave Spring. They had daddies who ran peach orchards, raised cows, or owned the town furniture store.

One girl said, "Chip's from Hot-lanta!"

Little do they know, I thought. *Oh, that's right, I'm a drama major. Fake it till you make it, or die trying.*

Oh, but being in a dorm with girls my same age was like having the best family in the world. We had a curfew of 11:15 p.m and drinking was prohibited, which was fine with me.

I was so happy just to be there and had nothing to rebel against, as did a girl named Rochelle, two doors down the hall, who had brought a bottle of vodka and started mixing up Moscow mules the second night.

In the meantime, I was living in mortal fear, so much so, I jumped every time the hall phone rang. I was afraid they'd call my name and it would be Mother saying I had to come home to go to court because of the law suit she'd gotten stuck with.

How could we have landed in such a misfortune?

~

It had all started back on the Fourth of July, when Mother drove to a little food market on Lee Street after supper because I was dying for a watermelon. On the way home a car sped through a stop sign and hit the car in front of us. The cars were spinning around. SCREECH! CRASH, BANG!

As Mother was trying to steer around the spinning cars and on through the intersection, Mother's car was hit, too. She slammed into the curb. Mother was knocked into the steering wheel, and my knee jammed into the dashboard.

I heard screams. I was afraid to get out. Porch lights came on. People started coming out of their houses. Someone said they saw the driver take off running. We just sat there. Finally Mother and I got out and walked to the intersection. A woman had been thrown out of the car. I saw her limp body lying in the gutter under the street light, her head on the curb with blood coming out of her ear. I heard someone say she was dead.

The words 'she's dead' echoed, because someone else would ask it, again, "Is she dead?"

"Lord, yes! She's dead."

I stood there with the alarmed bystanders waiting for the police, huddled against Mother in the July dampness, hearing the crying and moaning from the other three passengers suffering from their injuries and uttering distressed moans over the dead woman.

A young woman's life was gone now, and mine was just beginning. I was reminded again how quickly things could change, like with that wreck my Grandma had on Lee Street, not too far from here—a car wreck that changed her life forever and led to my Grandfather putting a bullet though his head soon after.

Someone said, "He must've been drunk. I saw him running."

We drove home in shock, and I never ever wanted to drive. Our injuries were minor. Mother found out that the fleeing driver wasn't the owner, and also that the car wasn't even insured.

A month went by, and one day in August we came home from work together and found a light blue summons stuck in the screen door.

Oh, my God! Mother was being sued for $134,000! I didn't know you could *be* sued for that much money, especially when you didn't have it.

I wanted to scream, or just collapse on the floor in a puddle, but I didn't. Mother and I just sat there together on the divan and read the summons, over and over, like a death sentence. Mother kept sighing so many of her, 'Hee-mee's!' and saying, "I always knew I'd end up in the poor house."

My life was ruined at seventeen—the month before I was to go off to college. I went around in a stupor.

My dream. Gone.

Mother went to a lawyer. He said I should go on to college and wait for the court trial.

That's when I started living in mortal fear. I knew it would all end soon and I would get that fatal phone call—that I'd have to go back home and go to work.

~

However, eighty miles away, mortal fear can temporarily be forgotten when one is practically skipping down Ag Hill with the excitement and trepidation of a new beginning, heading for my first class in French.

The next class was in the drama department in the basement of the Fine Arts building with a lab theater and a big shop just behind the huge auditorium stage. There were three main professors and only four new girls as freshman drama majors.

In the huge workshop our teacher gave us a tour of hammers, bins of nails, rolls of canvas, and paint brushes that must always go back *exactly* where they came from. I was surprised to learn that a drama major must work fifteen hours every quarter on costumes or scenery for the upcoming production.

Later that first week I found myself on my hands and knees, learning how to hammer in a clout nail. I was building a butt joint of three-inch rails of white pine to make a flat for the set of the Fall theater production, *Mrs. McThing*.

I never expected college to be, of all things, doing what I loved—building stuff. On the other hand, I was too afraid of rejection to audition for any productions, or maybe I did, but wasn't cast.

~

During the holidays, it was good to see my boyfriend Richard and chat with friends at Clyatt's Drug Store after church, but three months on my own had already changed me.

It wasn't just about figuring out how to get laundry done or managing a bit of spending money, or keeping up with classes. In spite of my average grades, I'd found I could hold my own within an entirely new social and educational order. I sensed a deeper quality being tapped into, one I would discover years later.

I was still the smiling girdled-and-gloved girl in Clyatt's Drug Store, but the talk was with the boys who were freshmen at Georgia Tech, laughing over the Georgia Bulldogs losing again.

Mother and I began our weary bit of Christmas, arguing over which tree to buy from the corner lot in West End, strung with lights and smelling of pine. We drove home with the tree sticking out of the trunk, instead of the two of us carrying it for a mile, as we'd done for so many years when we didn't have a car.

We set it up in the living room. I unrolled some cotton to put around the red-and-green metal stand. Mother brought out the thin cardboard boxes of ornaments and lights. She'd already been to the dime store to buy the obligatory box of silver tinsel. We began hanging the same old red and blue balls and the glass pine cone, unwrapping the fragile red-and-silver cardinal on a spring that clipped onto the branch of this year's short-needled spruce pine.

That first Christmas back home I felt a growing disparity between us. The tentacles of a clinging vine were loosening, hanging alone in the chilly winds of independence and self-preservation. I argued or had an opinion on everthing. I felt so superior and self-righteous, like some disease had taking over my mind.

Color us pathetic, the color of red and green mixed together into a muddy brown.

At least we could watch Ed Sullivan together.

As I looked at the two or three dinky gifts under the tree, I had a sudden realization that *no* present under *any* tree could ever bring me what I wanted most—permanent happiness—or at least something that would never disappoint me, ever again, *ever*, and it didn't come wrapped in a package.

And it didn't seem to be Richard either, though it was nice to go with him to a movie during the holidays. I couldn't see myself marrying him.

No, it was about finding a place where I belonged. I was eager to get back to my friends at the dorm.

~

I knew the college routine now, and I was happy to have Mother drop me off in the parking lot. I eagerly lugged my suitcase up three flights of stairs to greet everyone—like Jessica across the hall, an art major who sketched hands every night in a little spiral sketchbook; Claudette from Miami with a long scar on her upper arm who was majoring in Business; little Sally Jo who practiced the violin and was rumored to have put in two tampons; and Anne from Tignall, Georgia, who played trumpet in The Redcoat Band.

I'm sure I didn't audition for *Macbeth*, the winter quarter production. My mind just wasn't wired to understand Shakespeare, even though we had to memorize the witches' passage from *Macbeth* in high school. I was digging my own grave—*fire burn, and cauldron bubble*—caught in a swirling vortex of intimidation and fear of rejection.

One afternoon during that quarter, the technical director, Mr. Nole came into our acting class. He explained that they needed drumbeats for one of the scenes in *Macbeth,* and asked if anyone could play the kettle drums. The task sounded easy and fun. I knew nothing about kettle drums, except seeing them from the balcony of the Fox Theater during the free summer pops concerts.

I raised my hand.

(One reason I love writing this book is that when I see myself raising my hand in the lab theater, like a fool, I want to say, "That is so ME!" And it feels good to know that, and to be able to both laugh and cry at that eighteen-year-old lured into action because of the intoxicating effects of music and sound and action. Looking back, I see that once in a while I was right to raise my hand, like a wise fool in a fairy tale.)

"Technical rehearsals for *Macbeth* begin Sunday night," Mr. Nole reminded me. I was beginning to wonder if I'd made a huge mistake.

When I arrived backstage, there was a big kettle drum with a copper rim and two mallets lying on top which I immediately picked up to softly pummel. I was delighted. I was given the script pages to underline exactly which lines the *drums of Dunsenain* came in on. The stage manager would also cue me.

At the next rehearsal Mr. Nole had added a long sheet of aluminum and fashioned a wooden handle, 'flying' it from the lofty ceiling. So now I had two assignments: thunder *and* lightning.

Then it was opening night of *Macbeth.*

Curtain up.

I was perched on a folding chair in the offstage darkness, watching the witches climb up and down their backstage ladder, waiting for my cue. I enthusiastically pummeled the drums with soft mallets, and yanked the sheet of aluminum with a rough whip-like motion back and forth, intermittently, until the action was over.

I loved all of it. This was the beginning of the happiness I had longed for, and a feeling of belonging.

I ate meals at Snelling Hall dining room on a meal ticket, bought Pall Malls at the Jenny Belle Grill. I spent a lot of wasted hours smoking and bidding wrong at bridge. Glass ashtrays overflowed with lipstick-smeared cigarette butts. Music from someone's radio or phonograph was in the background.

The songs I remember most: "Shake Rattle and Roll," "Rock Around the Clock," "Sh-Boom," "Hearts of Stone," "Sincerely," "Mr. Sandman," and "Teach Me Tonight."

Those were the crazy days of panty raids, when freshmen boys in crew cuts and rat caps came parading over to the Myers Hall quadrangle at night with their shirttails hanging down over their undershorts, hoping a few girls (not me) would throw down their panties from the windows.

~

All too soon the school year ended. Mother rumbled her '49 Ford back to help me load up everything. I said goodbye to one of the happiest years I'd ever had. This lonely, only child had a family of friends on the third floor of Center Myers. This mediocre student had a fine year of learning about a lot of aspects of the theater, and an introduction to what higher education was about.

I had been yearning to give my heart and soul to *something*, and here it was—in that little college town of seven hills—Athens, Georgia. I loved the egalitarian feeling of the dorm, the thrill of helping put on a play every quarter. I loved feeling part of a big university, where hitchhiking to classes became a way of life. If I had died after that freshman year of college, I would have died happy.

I didn't want to go back home for the entire summer—I even dreaded it. Yet part of me was glad to be sitting next to Mother with the backseat piled to the roof with shoe boxes and hat boxes, feeling the relief that finals were over.

Then somewhere near Stone Mountain, on the outskirts of Atlanta, Mother said, "Shug, I've been waiting to tell you until school was out. The lawsuit's not settled. The trial's coming up soon."

~

SET BACK

Oh, yea gods! I had actually let myself forget about the lawsuit, as if it had all dissolved or something, and Mother had just forgotten to tell me.

I slumped in my seat, withdrawing the rest of the way home, seeing my hopes and dreams dry up. I remember thinking that we must be *fated*, like in the tragedies I'd been reading about—just destined to have something go wrong.

The worst thing was coming home to face those three rooms of dusty furniture that didn't fit and that bare light bulb in the cluttered bedroom. The thought of anyone ever coming to visit me on Holderness Street and seeing the mess was even worse now. I tried to cheer myself up, thinking, well, at least you had one good life-changing year.

On Monday morning Mother cooked eggs and bacon and left some for me and was off to work. I slept until noon. I sat quietly at the kitchen table, embarrassed to think of smoking a cigarette at home, so I didn't.

It was hot. Everything was depressing. I didn't want to call anyone. I was thinking that I wanted to get out of the house. The iron sat upright on the scorched ironing board pad, so I heated it and pressed a wrinkled pinkish chambray sheath dress I'd trimmed in rick-rack because I was too lazy to make a facing for the neck. I put on flats and walked to the bus stop, hoping to get a job right away because I wanted to be out of the house as much as possible.

But my heart didn't want my college experience to end so quickly. I didn't want to go to work, either, truth be told. After getting off the bus at Five Points in downtown Atlanta, I walked down to the Atlanta Division of the University of Georgia.

I kept thinking about how much I wanted to succeed at something, longing for someone to discover what I was good at and point me in the right direction.

I found the admissions office and looked through their summer class schedule sitting at a table in the snack area, where I lit up a cigarette.

I had one year of college and felt so sophisticated now. I *was* the new me, *Chip Ashurst*. I knew I could transfer credits if I ever did get to go back. I could live at home and tuition was $45.

I enrolled.

Mother sighed and deposited $100 in my checking account. The following Monday I was eager to get up early, get dressed and walk to the bus stop. Riding the trolley downtown, a burst of happiness throbbed in my stomach, like being in love. Once again I might finish college, be somebody, maybe even someone noteworthy.

In my French 104 class, I was introduced to a parable—*Le Jongleur de Notre Dame* with the English and French version in the same book. This is how I remember the moving tale.

A poor, simple juggler quietly slips into the Notre Dame Cathedral to make an offering. He has no money, so he rolls out his little carpet in front of the statue of Mary and begins his juggling routine. The priests discover this rude spectacle and come down the aisle to oust him, but suddenly they stop, look up at the statue of Mary and see tears streaming down her smooth stone cheeks.

I identified with that earnest little juggler, feeling his plight, knowing he didn't feel he belonged in that beautiful cathedral, yet wanting to be there to give his simple talents in devotion. His sincerity felt like my sincerity, happy to wait offstage to perform my improvisational playing of the kettle drums in *Macbeth*, and maybe never becoming good enough for much more.

~

That summer Mother bought us season tickets to the musicals at the outdoor theater at Chastain Park. Oh, I have Mother to thank for buying that car, now, and for finding the money for such extravagant tickets. We saw *The Merry Widow, Annie Get Your Gun,* Janet Blair playing Nellie Forbush in *South Pacific,* and Ray Bolger in *Charlie's Aunt.*

And what a relief from the growing tension between us, just to be sitting together outside in the night air, *under the stars*, as it was billed, on the hard flat stones of the amphitheater like the Greek theaters I had been reading about. Mother loved it, too, and we could talk about the music, and the songs, and laugh on the way home in the darkness of the old Ford.

~

The summer dragged on. I remember one hot summer night Mother and I were sitting outside together on the porch after dark, listening to the city crickets, swatting an occasional mosquito. We were on a small wooden settee for two with the seat covered in a crackly black oil cloth. I was telling her about college. I don't know if I told her about my crush on Dr. P., our acting teacher, but it was on my mind.

Mother was always saying 'be a sweet girl,' and her words were on my mind as I was thinking about that movie, *My Foolish Heart*, which had made such a huge impression on me; that movie and the music were woven into me like some kind of romantic moral fiber. In the movie Susan Hayward winds up marrying the wrong man because she got pregnant.

"I was a nice girl, wasn't I?" says Susan Hayward.

(In fact: These are J. D. Salinger's words from his short story, *Uncle Wiggly in Connecticut* from which the movie, *My Foolish Heart,* was based.)

I wanted to stay that nice girl, too, but I'd already had some thoughts that if Dr. P. asked me to visit his garage apartment, maybe I would, as the curiosity of my own sexuality was brimming like sparkles of dew—fresh, unformed, and pure.

What I remember is saying to Mother, "I wouldn't want to marry any man that would want to marry *me* . . . ."

I didn't finish the sentence, because it would hurt too much to say it out loud. But the rest of it ended, " . . . that would want to marry me, living in a place like this!"

~

And then I saw an ad in *The Atlanta Journal* about auditions for a TV hostess for Romper Room School. *Oh, this is it!* My lucky chance. My break. This is the *deus ex machina* I'd just learned about.

I'd had one year of drama, and they would naturally want me. I could even report that I'd already appeared on TV. I'd have the start I'd been hoping for, because this job would lead to something bigger and better and soon . . . .very soon . . .

I was dreaming all that as I rode the bus to the TV station auditions, wearing a black sheath dress, white gloves, a girdle, and a wide black picture hat. I was sure of getting this job. I kept thinking this was what my year of drama had prepared me for, and the stupid lawsuit wouldn't matter because I'd be making real money. I saw my entire world opening up into the magical life I'd always dreamed of.

At the TV station I stood in a crowded hallway with many other girls; some weren't nearly as pretty as I, but others had teaching backgrounds.

Teaching? I thought we were entertaining children with learning games.

I had watched the Romper Room TV program—the Do-Bee children followed the teacher's animated directions. In my interview I was happy to reply, "Yes, I have *taught*—in Vacation Bible School."

I was never even called back. And I just couldn't figure it out. I really couldn't. *How could they not choose me?*

With all my sophomoric ignorance and inflated self-worth, I was still defending an ego the size of the Eiffel Tower.

~

As August neared, a trial date had been set for October. *Oh, Lord!* Mother started coaching me, because she'd just visited with her lawyer. Apparently he'd said something about my testifying.

Ye gods! Must I take the witness stand?

This news threw me into a tailspin. Suddenly I had a morbid fear of telling the truth, remembering that movie of someone being injected with sodium pentathol, "truth serum."

I felt a deathly chill.

To have to *tell the truth, the whole truth, and nothing but the truth* was like going before St. Peter to see if I'd be allowed into Heaven, and I'd have to admit to how utterly *low and worthless* I felt all the time.

My whole life was a lie. One big cover-up.

Every night at supper, we would argue over the accident.

Poor Mother! Stuck with this recalcitrant daughter about to convict her own mother on the witness stand.

"Mother, you shouldn't have swerved to try to go around the other cars!" I said.

"Shug, I did the best I could."

I could feel for her, but I had no way to separate my own desperate feelings.

"I know I wasn't going over fifteen miles an hour," she repeated.

The next evening at supper, we would wrangle all over again.

"I always said I'd end up in the poorhouse," Mother moaned again at the kitchen table.

The trial hung over us like a death sentence.

~

Then came the Fall of utter disappointment. Come September, I turned nineteen, and I didn't get to return to school for my sophomore year. The trial was imminent. $134,000 was looming, so I found a job.

It was easy to get a billing clerk job with the Retail Credit Company where the entire third floor was nothing but a roomful of desks and young girls.

My life had come down to this: sorting boxes and boxes and boxes of Retail Credit billing invoices in a huge wooden tray that fit at a slant in the desk drawer. We sorted each paper invoice by its six digit number into the wooden bins. ten slots across, and ten down. I spent all of October smoking, biting my nails, and filing credit invoices.

My drama friend, Dorothy McConkey, told me she was in *The Lady's Not For Burning*. I knew I didn't want that kind of role, or have her desire to be an actress, or her background in high school one-acts, much less her ability. I was in love with the tinsel glamour of show business that shines in the broad realm of *stardom* with dreams of my name in lights.

Now, everything I'd silently dreamed was slowly fading to black. I accepted my fate without a whimper this time.

Mother came home one night in October and announced that the trial was still on for next week.

Oh, Lord!

I braced myself again. I didn't know if I could flat out lie, because I really felt I was an honest person and had never cheated or stolen anything, and I really *did* think Mother could've handled the car better and not been '*negligent.*'

And suddenly—it was all over—everything had been settled out of court. Mother didn't have to pay anything!

I never understood it all, but, Hallelujah, I could go back to school.

~

In January, 1956, I was giddy with excitement riding the bus to join my class for winter quarter. I was charting my course again, though I couldn't yet see beyond the boundaries of my own narrow boat—maybe I never would—but for now, I had a second chance.

All the nameless things I'd been longing for seemed to be at the end of that long bus ride back to Athens, Georgia. As the Greyhound bus driver shifted into low gear grinding up the hill to the light at Pulaski Street just before the bus station, tears of joy rolled down my cheeks.

Somewhere deep inside, in that *knowing cave where the bones reside*, I knew I was on the road to the truth of my life. I was happy with a gratitude I'd never experienced before, to be back where I belonged: the campus of the University of Georgia.

That joyous "coming home" feeling would strangely reoccur anytime I was making that uphill approach into town to the bus station on Broad Street.

Like coming home to myself.

~

Chapter 17

Into the Mainstream

I STEPPED OFF THE BUS with memories of last year's laughter and the friendship of those freshmen girls, but I arrived at my dorm, Rutherford Hall, on a wintry day in January and there was no one around. The dorm room doors stayed shut. There was no one to greet me. I was a character lugging a suitcase down an ancient, dimly lit hallway, alone, looking for a room number.

The first two nights I tossed and turned in the narrow dorm bed. I don't even remember my roommate. Even though I was glad to take a class in drama, I felt I'd fallen behind and the pressure to make something of myself gnawed at me in the dingy dorm room. So I filled out a winter rush card.

I must be nuts! I thought. *How will Mother pay for this?*

~

Soon I was in the middle of panhellenic rush, walking up the wide entries of each of those beautiful houses. I felt like a fraud.

One sorority sent me a pledge invitation. I said 'yes,' and joined the other pledges to be greeted by our new "sisters."

Back in my dark dorm room, I sighed because I wasn't as happy as I thought I'd be.

Oh, Lord, what have I done?

I wrote Mother that I'd been invited to join a sorority and told her the cost. She sent a check to cover a pledge pin and fees.

How did she ever manage it? I took so much for granted.

Soon I was wearing a pledge pin and attending pledge meetings every Monday night, but even with that and being back in school working on a new play, I was lonely in the dorm.

I tried playing bridge again, but after a few hands of carelessly counting cards, I was not a welcomed partner, so I wandered down to the dark dorm basement and discovered an old piano. No one was ever down there, so I plinked around, humming notes in my head, dreaming—*maybe I could write a musical—yes, that's what I'd love to do!*

I immediately felt a release of tension just playing some chords and then playing my old song "Yesterday's Love." Music transformed my loneliness into a dreamy pleasure. In that dark basement I felt the exhilaration of a new song stirring inside me, unfolding into the melody of an opening number, imitating a slow rhythm like something from *An American in Paris.*

I thought of a musical that took place on a boat, *The U.S.S. Periwinkle*, with a bunch of students going to Europe having student romances. I called it "Periwinkle Blues."

It was just another idea that kept me afloat long enough for another day of hope, and never went anywhere.

~

Do you remember those beautiful houses I was swooning over, a little over a year ago in the Panhellenic booklet?

In spring quarter I am living in one!

Lo and behold, a vacancy opened up in the sorority house. Spring quarter Mother was dropping me off at a big beautiful house with white Corinthian columns, white swings, and rockers that sat on a wide wrap-around porch. There was a curved driveway going under a sheltered portico known as a carriage-landing.

Every time I turned the knob of the heavy beveled glass front door, it was as if I was stepping into the set of *Gone with the Wind*, except that it was the 1950s, with girls in sweaters and loafers and tight skirts with a split up the back, chattering about boyfriends and tests—girls that wore heels and hats and girdles and gloves to football games and church on Sundays.

I lived there, but I didn't belong there. I was more at home helping with the next theater production.

Oh, but living in that beautiful house, walking up and down an elegant curved staircase every day, having a nice address, wearing a sorority pin with pearls—what a way to end my sophomore year.

Some dreams do come true—even if they last just long enough for tomorrow, or for reality to set in.

When the quarter was over I was back in three messy rooms at home where I could be me, even if I didn't like myself. At least I didn't have to pretend I was someone else.

~

In my junior year, I was cast in a University Theater production as Millie in *Picnic*, the teenage sister: an intelligent, rambunctious, and ambitious girl frustrated with living in the shadow of her sister and not being seen for her own talents.

After weeks of rehearsal, it was opening night. *Imagine that!* I thought to myself. *I'm in a play on the stage of Fine Arts.*

As the curtain went up on *Picnic*, I entered through a screen door onto a small porch, my hair in a ponytail, dressed in my own rolled-up jeans and saddle-oxfords. I sat on the edge of the porch facing the audience. A spotlight from the balcony was streaming in my eyes and I saw a real theater audience for the first time. I was all alone on stage, just me and the spotlight.

I felt completely at home.

Next, I reached under the steps for a pack of my own cigarettes—which was now a *prop*—and lit up one on stage. I had a few lines with Bomber, the paper boy—then, hearing footsteps, I quickly stubbed out the cigarette and waved away the smoke. The audience giggled.

I loved it! I was not just "acting" believable, I *was* believable. All I needed were a few good lines or "stage business," and I was in my element.

After that scene I quickly changed out of the rolled-up jeans and into the next of three costumes—all of which were mine. In the "Neewollah" dance scene, (Halloween spelled backwards), I had my hair down and wore a black cotton sleeveless dress with small flowers imprinted. Monte Markham, a transfer student, was handsomely playing bare-chested Hal with jeans tucked in his boots. And there was the wonderful music, "Moonglow" and the "Picnic Theme."

In the final scene, I wore my lavender gingham gathered skirt with a bib and a white blouse underneath, loafers and books tucked under my arm and, as Millie, I exited on a line about writing something so good, it would knock everyone's socks off!

An English professor reviewed the play and wrote, *"Miss Ashurst, as Millie, was consistently the finest actor in the play."* I was astonished and bought an extra copy and sent it to Mother.

~

I thought about sending the review to my father.

I remember that contemplative moment after my first success. I was in my bunk bed that afternoon since none of my roommates had come back from class.

I sat looking at that *Picnic* review.

Part of me wanted to think that if my father read it—*his daughter, Miss Ashurst*—followed by a glowing account of my performance, that my father might come and visit me. The other part of me didn't want to be disappointed, rationalizing that this was just a minor part in an inconsequential college play.

Maybe I should just wait, for now. I thought. *Maybe I'll do something even bigger—so big, he'll have to come see me.*

I underlined the "good part" of the review and tucked it away in an envelope and have kept it for over fifty years.

~

One of six roommates, Charlene, an only child, had been to New York during the summer and heard a musician named Jimmy Guiffry at the Village Vanguard. I longed to go a coffee house in Greenwich Village in New York to hear poetry readings in a brick-walled cellar with beatniks playing bongos.

Charlene played her new album of jazz arrangements from *My Fair Lady*. I'd never heard Andre Previn's piano style of Broadway jazz. I found myself drawn to the trio's smooth pulse—the sound of a heartbeat and a sob together—and the joy of expressing it.

The next afternoon I went to the downtown record store on Lumpkin Street and bought my first jazz record.

Had to!

You know one of those *had to* moments? Some deep urge is so irrestible, squeezing your heart and soul into ambrosia, that you simply must follow up. In the record store I listened to a lot of records and found the perfect 45-rpm record called *Lullaby of Broadway*, played by eight different jazz groups. One of the pianist was a woman, Barbara Carroll. A *woman* playing jazz! That's what I wanted to do. I listened to it again and again on my little phonograph.

I went downstairs to the grand piano in the living room and picked out some jazz chords. They soothed a restlessness and spoke to heartache and fulfillment.

That quarter Charlene and I wrote a parody of *The Hit Parade* show for Panhellenic Stunt Night. I bought a baritone ukelele at Chick Piano Company for accompaniment. We made a replica of our famous Georgia Arches from a refrigerator carton. Our first number was "It's Athens in the Rain," a soft shoe tap with twirling umbrellas and raincoats on the Fine Arts Stage. Then we staged a registration table scene and six girls sang:

> **"I never felt more like singin' the blues,**
> **'Cause I never thought that I'd ever lose**
> **... my I. D. Card!**
> **You Got Me Singin' the Blues."**

The student audience howled with laughter.
Our sorority won!

The judges named me as outstanding performer. No one in the drama department was even there. I figured it wouldn't mean anything to them, anyway. The Drama department produced plays by Albee, Shaw, Shakespeare, T. S. Eliot, and Giradoux.

"Trite!" I could hear my drama professors saying.

~

Everything changed in the spring of 1957.

I became sorority president.

President! Good Lord, what were the alums thinking?

Two married alums had cornered me one afternoon under the backporch stairs and said there was no other sister available.

That's how it happened—a lot of prestige, responsibility and pressure dumped on me. I became a leader, by default. I still don't know what they saw in me.

How would I keep up with my classes? How could I manage the extra meetings? How could I attend to the new drama assignments of increasing complexity? I had no one to talk to about any of this—just mental pandemonium—biting my nails even more, and smoking, and eating too much, because underneath I knew I was a *nobody* from *nowhere-lane*.

When I went home I took it all out on Mother.

I said, "I just wish we could *move!*"

Mother looked stunned and perplexed, like *What is this child going to demand next?*

"You know, Mother, " I whined, "now that I'm president."

Poor Mother! I sort of rationalized that that's what I'd do if I had *me* as a daughter.

(I learned later that when Mother went to a new job at Piedmont Life, she had cashed in her thirteen-year retirement money from Mutual of Omaha to pay for the rest of my junior year.)

Not long after that Mother wrote that she'd heard of an available apartment on Peachtree Street near her new office.

I couldn't believe it!

Oh, but I didn't want to get my hopes up too much about living somewhere else. And then, bless her heart, while I was in school, Mother had our furniture moved into a yellowish brick apartment building at 1215 Peachtree Street.

Every time I filled out a change of address form, I was weirdly and wildly happy. To have lived for nineteen years in the same rotting house, and now to think we had a new little apartment on Peachtree Street, was simply unbelievable.

I didn't even care what it looked like. I felt like I could handle anything with this boost in social status, as if maybe I *did* deserve the bit of recognition I'd received.

Mother drove over to Athens to take me home for that first weekend in our new apartment. There was a long wide elegant walkway up to the building entrance. The artsy Tenth Street area was two blocks away where there was an art movie theater, a small art gallery, and a little playhouse theater.

Even though it wasn't a wonderful residential house like Aunt Gladys had in Buckhead, or Uncle Oscar's home on Piedmont Road, at least when someone asked where I lived, I didn't have to say West End with a fake, tense smile.

~

That summer I started my Kelly Girl temporary job assignments. After work I went looking for material since we had nothing to put in the small foyer with its resounding hardwood floors and glass French doors leading into the living room.

I rented a sewing machine and found some champagne-colored shantung on sale and made a cover for that old day-bed, then made pillow slips for a couple of musty pillows, hoping it looked decent enough for the entry.

"Set decorations," I called it. *"This is Peachtree Street—that's what really counts."*

After the decorating project was done I started making a strapless sheath dress in emerald green with emerald green lace overlay and spaghetti straps, envisioning wearing it somewhere special my senior year.

Every day I felt like a new person making my entrance into the world walking out that long wide walkway to the bus stop in flats or heels, depending on the temporary job assignment.

~

I remember this one incident. I was walking toward the bus stop on the corner of Peachtree Street by Davison-Paxon's Department Store just as a busload of Shriners was slowing down. They started hanging out the windows in their red Shriner's hats with gold tassels, ogling, waggling their tongues, and whistling.

"Look at that *Georgia Peach*," said one. "That's some *tomato*!" said another.

I remember that day so well. I wasn't wearing anything special, just a two-piece yellow-and-brown plaid nubby cotton dress with a gathered skirt and flats. I turned and smiled and felt flattered, but then ducked my head and walked on.

When you are blessed with a pretty smile, it *does* light up the world and *is* a gift. But on that day, when I smiled, I felt good and bad at the same time.

~

Reflecting on that day, I remember those grown men hanging out the bus windows, whistling, showing off in front of their peers, making boyish sexual innuendoes to *each other*, and *to me*—remarks they would never make back home. I see now that they could act out being powerful just by shouting their titillating catcalls, thus making me an object to be both flattered and degraded.

I've come to think that moments like that which continue to linger vividly and disturb my psyche are connected to that *knowing cave* I spoke of earlier. A veil is lifted for a moment and you *know* some greater truth in your *bones*. I think it's a blend of conscious awareness, along with the collective unconscious.

And isn't it interesting that it was the red Turkish caps, which I associate with harems—*harms to my soul*—that was giving me warning about my state of innocence that day.

It was the same awareness I began to have at the beginning of puberty, sprouting breasts and having the neighborhood boys suddenly show up at Lester's basketball goal. And it was the same awareness about those Lions Club men watching our little singing duo, at fifteen, as we sang in sarongs, barefoot.

I was living out a modern day fairy tale experience of Little Red Riding Hood with Lions and Shriners, ready to devour a girl child, should she not be wary and protect herself.

I've come to realize that each *felt* experience in my life had more layers of meaning than I was able to grasp at twenty.

~

Later that summer, on a hot August day, I'd walked to Tenth Street and was coming back from seeing a boring art movie, *Kontiki*, about a man on a raft for days and days.

Mother looked serious. "Come in here, I need to tell you something."

She sat on the bed covered with a nubby white chenille bedspread. Reading Mother's face, I remember feeling my stomach sink with anxiety. Reaching for my baritone ukelele I sat on the end of the bed, strumming it.

"Mother is having some problems at work," she said. "They're putting all billing on IBM cards, and it's hard for me to read them, and I'm not fast enough."

Oh, Lord, I don't want to hear this!

"I'm not sure how long I can keep this job," she said. "And this apartment is just too much for me to pay for."

A few tears trickled down from under her glasses.

Oh, Please don't say it!

"Shug, I'm gonna have to move us back to Holderness Street."

I just kept strumming slowly.

"Stop that!" said Mother restraining her anger. "My eyes are bad. I can't work that fast," she repeated. "We're gonna have to move back."

~

Oh, Lord, forgive me. I didn't hug her. I didn't say I'm sorry. I couldn't dredge up any sympathy, whatsoever, that day. I didn't care one whit about Mother's problem. All I could think of was— you know who—me.

~

Chapter 18

Hold onto Your Dreams

OH, THOSE FEW MONTHS OF PEACHTREE HEAVEN. And then we moved back—though I don't remember anything about it. I've totally repressed it all. To have come so far, and now, when I returned to school, I could feel my cheeks burning as I filled out a change of address card from Peachtree Street back to Holderness Street.

Color me blue. *A blue tomato.*

Back on Holderness Street, I didn't even have time to cry because it was September, and we were cramming my clothes and shoeboxes into the backseat, again, with two hatboxes and a ukelele piled on top. I was about to turn twenty-one. Mother started up the Ford engine. As she eased away from the curb, I heard those twin mufflers rumbling.

"Here we go, Shug, your senior year." she said with a smile.

~

You could color me a bright, hopeful yellow, too, because more than anything, I loved writing skits and making up song parodies for rush. This year we were doing songs from *South Pacific*: "Bloody Mary" and "There's Nothing Like a Dame."

Oh, but school work was a nightmare. I had three quarters of play production. I chose *Light Up the Sky* by Moss Hart and had to make a prompt book, a set design, blocking, write in sound and light cues, make a poster design, and a publicity plan.

For directing class, I teamed up with my friend Dorothy McConkey to co-direct a one-act, *Chi-Chi*, by Pirandello, helping with the set, choosing the music, and running the lights.

~

The University Theater's first production was *A Streetcar Named Desire*. I hadn't even liked the movie with Marlon Brando acting like a thug, being so mean and brutish to Vivien Leigh.

Holy Cow! I was cast as Stella.

Dorothy was cast as Blanche. Monte played Stanley.

Reading the script I saw that in the first scene Stella appears in a slip.

Ye gods! A slip!

I could already feel the spotlight on me and the audience gasping, or gaping.

Heavens to Betsy! I can't do it. What would Mother say?

I kept putting off saying anything to the director, but finally I said, "I can't be in a slip, I'd be too embarrassed."

"WHAT!!" he barked. "Oh, my God!"

He was already exasperated with me for not learning my lines on time. I was scared to death that I would just ruin everything. He explained that the script *called* for it, that the *slip* was a *costume*—not *me* in my *underwear,* and that's what made this Tennessee Williams play authentic.

Already I'd received a bruise from a kitchen scene when Stanley pushes Stella. With consternation I gave in and wore a half slip under my whole slip, so I wouldn't feel so exposed.

On opening night when the curtain went up, I was stretched out on a chaise lounge, in my slip-and-a-half, eating a bag of Hershey kisses. The chaise was angled near the edge of the stage, so I took a side glance at the audience during one of Stanley's speeches. I saw the face of a local bank officer who had always smiled at me whenever I'd visit the local bank. There he was on the second row, the spill of the footlights lighting up his face.

When I first stood up, I could feel his awed look, staring up at Stella in a slip. And, *folks, you won't believe this*—as they say —his name was J. Smiley Wolfe. I can still see it engraved on that little brass nameplate on his desk at the bank.

All the sexual innuendos Tennessee Williams wrote were way over my head. My friend Dorothy was marvelous as Blanche. I knew what a good actress was—and it wasn't me.

~

Now let me tell you about what I learned from a rehearsal scene. My character, Stella, must wait at the top of eight stairs behind a painted flat on a four-by-four platform, listening for her cue.

(Chip Ashurst, Monte Markham, unidentified poker players. University of Georgia Pandora Yearbook)

"Stel-l-a . . . Stel-l-a!" shouts Monte Markham playing Stanley.

"Wait . . . wait!" shouts the director, from the darkness of the theater, meaning *don't come down yet*.

"Stel-l-a-a-a! . . ."

"Wait! . . . wait . . . . now!" he directs.

Then I start down the stairs.

"Slowly. . . slow-ly," he hisses . . . then, "No! No!"

And then we must do it again . . . and again.

Ye gods! I am never slow enough for him!

Now it's the final dress rehearsal. I am again perched on my off-stage platform, wearing a maternity top now, with a small pillow strapped under it.

In my literal-minded head I kept thinking, *no one in their right mind would ever come down stairs that slowly, even if they were pregnant.*

Stanley begins his "Stella's" again, and I wait for the third one . . . and wait just a moment more . . . and then begin my slow descent.

I hear the director hissing from the dark auditorium, "Slow-ly . . . slow-ly, darling . . . slow-ly . . . don't rush!" And then from the darkness beyond the footlights, one final exasperated, "Slowly . . . GODDAMN IT! SLOWLY!"

~

I learned a lot about direction *and* art from that *Streetcar* scene. It's the pauses . . . the silences on stage and in a movie that build tension, that let the audience have time—and space—to wonder what the character will do—what they themselves would do.

That same artistic principle of allowing space would later be reflected in my own musical compositions and poetry and making one line paragraphs writing this book. Later I understood the character of Blanche Dubois—that the *soul itself* needs space.

Being in *A Streetcar Named Desire* was memorable for another reason, too. I remember Mr. Nole handing me a book with a photo of a lamp post in the French Quarter district of New Orleans, saying, "This is your assignment." He handed me a sheet of paper with a rectangle drawn, maybe twenty-four by twelve inches.

"Do a sketch of the wrought iron grillwork on the lamp post within this rectangle," he said. "Then trace it off and cut it out using the shop jigsaw. Then paint it black." And I did.

I was more proud of that French Quarter lamp post replica than I was of playing Stella.

~

Winter quarter I was stage manager for *Othello*. I executed forty-five sound cues and fifty-five lighting cues. I was good at this, and I liked it because I *was* good at it. I belonged backstage as much as onstage.

On the other hand, my Play Analysis class required analytical skills far beyond my abilities since I took everything literally.

Dr. P. kept asking, "What does the playwright mean?"

I didn't even begin to understand the satire of Moliere, but when Dr. P. paraphrased a line, it made more sense. It was stuff like that that made me feel downright stupid. Dr. P. was a patient teacher though, and good at giving examples.

I remember in one class session, Dr. P. was standing at the blackboard, drawing a diagram to make a point. It was just a long horizontal chalk line.

"This is a continuum," he said, as he drew a line through the center. He wrote *comedy* at one end, and *tragedy* at the other. He asked the class for examples. That was easy to see.

The sleeve of his dark blue suit had chalk dust on it as he erased *comedy* and changed out the opposites, to *realism* and *abstract,* then *conservative* and *liberal.*

A light bulb snapped on. That continuum helped me make a new kind of connection in my brain. Just that knowledge alone was so interesting that it made me feel better about myself because I could now literally "see" the relationship between different points of view. *(I believe I am one whose brain is wired to think in pictures better than words.)*

On another day in class he said, "Everything written isn't always true." I was dumbstruck. *What? Things written in books aren't always true!* That was another revelation.

Because Dr. P. treated me and all the other students with a friendly, respectful attitude, I was more open to learning. He also held individual conferences with each student. None of my other teachers ever did this, and I was both excited and scared to see him alone because I still had a huge crush on him.

In his tiny office cubicle, just large enough for his desk and a chair beside it, I sat bracing myself watching him look for my folder in his file drawer. No teacher had ever been so genuine, and that's why I couldn't help but be infatuated with him.

"What grade do you think you should get?" he asked me.

I was floored that he would put the responsibility for my grade on *me*. It irritated me that he wanted to make *me* think. I already knew what I'd made on my papers—mostly C's, except for one B. I got up enough courage to be honest, even though I knew it would make me look like a fool. I told him about the continuum, and how I didn't know until his class that things written in books weren't necessarily true.

"I think I should get a B," I said, "because I learned to think."

~

That last winter quarter cracked open my fundamentalist, narrow-minded thinking, born and bred into me. All this time I'd been a hard-headed weed of a person, skeptical of new ideas, making it tough to extricate the deep tap roots of prejudice.

Higher education had been like cultivation, breaking up that hard, compacted, resistant, Georgia red-clay brain. The insights from his class were a turning point. My assumptions were up for reexamination—but that would be a long time coming.

And I got a B.

~

And then it was spring quarter. My presidency was over. Dr. P. cast me as Elizabeth in a British play, Somerset Maugham's *The Circle*. ("Tennis, anyone?" is the famous line.)

The clever reviewer wrote something like this: "As the play wore on, Miss Ashurst's British accent waned, having completely crossed the Atlantic Ocean by Act III."

(Dorothy McConkey, Robert Weigle, Chip Ashurst, University of Georgia, 1959, Pandora Yearbook)

Oh, but I wore the most beautiful dress I'd ever owned—blue chiffon, mid-calf length, with iridescent sequins in the bodice—a Grace Kelly dress. Maybe Mother knew how important it was for me since this was my final play; she let me buy it on sale at *Muse's* for $50. I wish I had a picture of it, or had kept it forever.

~

Spring quarter was over—and four years, too.

I wish I could say some of my classwork or theater work was ever stunning or exceptional—or even original—but it wasn't. I just muddled through. Yet building sets and learning to use a jigsaw was a perfect fit for my natural talent for design.

However, the best moment in my college life had been singing my heart out with the ensemble of sorority sisters for Panhellenic Stunt Night. I can still hear the thunderous applause, and revel in the echo of cheers resounding in Fine Arts Auditorium. It was intoxicating to hear my name announced as the outstanding performer.

The applause was for the real me, Chip Ashurst.

That night I had realized the happiness and ecstasy of being where I belonged—writing and performing in musical theater.

Finishing four years of college was goal and my dream, and I had made it. College had added more to my life than I could ever have imagined. I became more than that Bachelor of Fine Arts degree I was awarded.

But what now?

What could I do with just a love for musical theater?

I couldn't even let myself think about the fact that I would love to be taking a bus to New York after college if my friend Dorothy had suggested it. I pictured us rooming together, like the sisters in the movie *My Sister Eileen* with Rosalind Russell, and me taking a typing job to help pay my half the rent, because I'd be near Broadway where I felt I really belonged. But Dorothy was taking a bank job in Atlanta.

Three weeks after graduation, I married a boy I'd met in my sophomore year.

~

Chapter 19

Betty Crocker Is Not Allowed to Scream!

THE BOY I MARRIED WAS FROM Hapeville, Georgia, near Atlanta. He was four years older than I and had the right look for someone majoring in personnel management—a crew cut, horn-rimmed glasses, khakis, Madras shirts, crew-neck sweaters, buttoned-down Oxford cloth shirts, and tasseled loafers.

He said we'd make a good match.

He drank Scotch in Poss's iced tea. I sipped on it and we made out in his blue Chevy and at his little apartment on Hill Street.

His father sorted mail for the Post Office on a train route from Atlanta to Jacksonville. His younger brother, Jimmy was married with a baby. His mother, Pearl, had blue eyes and white hair, taught Sunday School and played hymns on the piano. She grew up in Statham, Georgia and graduated from Lucy Cobb Normal School.

My husband-to-be "joined up" before graduating from high school, proud of being a waist-gunner on a B-29, though he never saw combat during the Korean War. He passed the GED and made it through college on the G. I. Bill and was the first in his family to graduate from college—so maybe he was right—we were a good match.

On paper—that is.

~

Larry and I met on campus at the student co-op, popular for cheap lunches like grilled pimiento cheese sandwiches, chili, and chocolate shakes. Since he was president of one of the smaller fraternities, I looked to him for support and suggestions.

One Sunday night we were parked in the sorority driveway. I was already thinking about Monday night's sorority meeting, brooding over making a little speech to the sisters and rehearsing it in my mind.

I told him I wanted to tone down the ugly rush comments. I told him that a sister had said at one rush meeting, "Chip never says anything bad about anyone," and that her remark had encouraged me to speak up. I said I would tell the sisters about being from West End in Atlanta, and say, 'let's not be so judgmental during rush, making insulting remarks about some girl we don't even know.'

As I was blurting out my own social deficits, I started to cry. I had never let myself be so honest with anyone. Tears flooded down my face spilling onto my pink angora sweater. He cradled me in his arms and held me in the darkness of his car. It felt so good. Maybe he felt that way, too.

He said I shouldn't give that little speech because it wouldn't do any good, and just make me look bad because the sisters that were spiteful wouldn't understand, anyway.

So I chickened out. But that brief shared experience of honesty and intimacy in the darkness of his car was our bonding moment.

My roommates were getting married. Here I was in my senior year and then what? I had no idea, so when Larry said we'd make a good match, I said yes.

Another reason for getting married I blame on *Cosmopolitan* magazine.

Yes. Cosmopolitan!

I had read an article that said that the average girl had had sex by age twenty-two. And I hadn't had sex. Petting had been especially exciting with Richard, and I was curious.

We got engaged at Christmas.

And then I had to tell Mother.

At supper, my stomach began churning as I sat across from her at that same old white painted table where I'd eaten so many meals; where earlier I'd been so excited about my singing adventures; where I'd once put blue food coloring in mashed potatoes, and Mother had said I had to eat them anyway; where I'd once drunk milk out of a tennis cup; and especially where I'd shown her my letter of acceptance to college.

It was hard to be back at that same kitchen table to tell Mother the *news* because my heart wasn't in it. A lump came in my throat.

"What *is it*, Shug?" said Mother.

"Larry asked me to marry him," I said, "so I guess I will."

I spoke with all the flatness of an open road to nowhere.

I don't remember her reply.

She was probably glad I was getting married because what would she do with me if I didn't? And what would I do with myself?

~

On a hot Saturday in June, 1958, his parents drove Mother over to Athens for our graduation. Afterwards, we gathered outside Sanford Stadium, peeling off our black robes, standing for those few minutes, smiling and laughing—a moment never to be forgotten by any of us. We were holding our diplomas, tucking in the mortarboard tassel for a keepsake. We'd made our parents proud and reached our goals. It was a good day, and now we were going to live out the American Dream.

Three weeks later, on July 2, 1958, I stood at the back of Gordon Street Baptist Church wearing a wedding dress borrowed from one of my sorority sisters. Mother charged our wedding bands on her Rich's account.

I watched as Sandra, my maid of honor, walked down the aisle before me. Uncle Harry, Aunt Clara's husband, stood by my side in a white dinner jacket, shifting his stork legs from foot to foot, waiting to give me away. And there I was, about to walk down that same aisle where I had 'joined the church' years earlier, with similar doubts about my committment.

(Mother, me, Sandra Brown, 1958)

To refresh your memory, I wrote: *Now, if the minister had asked me to commit myself to becoming a movie star, I would've run down the aisle of the Gordon Street Baptist Church and dropped to my knees, pledging to work myself to the bones, studying, sacrificing, doing anything, because that's where my heart was. My heart wasn't with Jesus. It was with show business.*

Well, my heart wasn't with marriage either. I was still in love with show business, but fate had cast me in the role of Betty Crocker, complete with a set of stainless steel mixing bowls, *some* silver, *some* crystal, *some* china, a Penguin stainless steel ice bucket, two chip-'n-dip sets, an empty recipe box, and a douche bag Mother had given me the night before.

I'd dreamed of having a honeymoon at the King and Prince Hotel on St. Simons Island, off the Georgia coast, but we didn't have the money. After a short stay at the Waldorf Motel, we returned to a little furnished garage apartment.

On Monday he went back to his new job selling life insurance. I'd just started as a receptionist for State Farm and had to suffer through the male claim's adjusters' innuendos about my honeymoon weekend.

I put a smile in my voice like Lucy Ricardo on *I Love Lucy* and answered the phone.

"State Farm Claim Office."

Then I manually typed in the long State Farm policy number on a teletype machine. Each key punched a hole in a thin strip of yellow teletype paper which I fed into a slot. When I pressed a button, something magically read the *click-click-clicks* and sent the message off to the home office in Jacksonville, Florida.

I could never type numbers, so I was really lousy. You can't erase a hole you've punched wrong. And you can't *see* what you've punched, unless you can read it like morse code, or Braille. You just have to start over again.

It was pretty easy to slip into the receptionist's role. The great improviser with a drama degree was at least *getting paid* for her acting job. And I liked sending off those urgent messages as it reminded me of using Captain Midnight's decoder badge.

At five o'clock I covered my typewriter, locked my desk and the supply cabinet. And then I was off to our cute little garage apartment, which I did love. It had a fireplace, pine paneling, a tiny kitchen, and a squeaky set of springs under the mattress.

You've heard the expression, "You've made your bed, now lie in it - squeaky mattress and all!" That's how I faced marriage as I stood waiting for the bus in Decatur, transferred to another bus, then got off two blocks from the apartment at a small grocery store.

I had made a grocery list for the first time in my life and bought ground beef for a meat loaf, an onion, two potatoes—to bake or mash—frozen spinach, canned pears, a loaf of bread, Jiffy yellow cake mix, and Jiffy corn muffin mix.

Lugging the sack of groceries in the August heat, I walked home in heels and a tight girdle, then dragged myself up the garage steps. I put the sack down on the small landing to fish out the key from my navy going-away purse. *Lord was it hot!* I turned on the fan, hoping to prepare the perfect meal for hubby.

The trouble was I had never cooked a meal except as a cooking assignment in ninth-grade Home Ec class with Mrs. Johnson. What I remember most in her class was that we must never say 'boiled eggs' because we must never *boil* an egg, just bring it *to* a boil, cover and simmer. Then they are correctly called *hard-cooked eggs*. We also made muffins, stewed apple halves, and a sauce made by melting little red cinnamon hearts to pour over the stewed apples.

Aunt Clara had given me a pink organdy apron of no use at all since it was so dainty I would never want to wipe my hands on it.

The thing is, after two or three weeks of being a housewife, I'd be all happy trying to cook up supper, but as soon as I heard my husband's footsteps coming up to the garage apartment, I froze, and all the charm vanished. I became stiff and cold. If he asked me how I was, I'd say, "I'm fine," in that bristly way that is a total lie that everyone accepts, if you know what I mean.

Every night after supper my husband was out making insurance calls. We didn't have a TV. I didn't know what to do with myself after I'd finished looking at the same *Family Circle* magazine, daydreaming of making a pineapple upside-down cake with those pretty red cherries in the center of pineapple rings.

I didn't know how miserable I was, so how could I be honest and tell somebody? I didn't call anyone—not Mother, or Sandra, or Dorothy, who was now working at a bank.

Proper Aunt Clara invited us over to play Canasta on a Sunday afternoon to get to know my new husband better. She allowed jovial Uncle Harry to break out his homemade blackberry wine.

I had moved from a wonderful college life, in which I felt challenged and valued, into a social planet that orbited around nine-to-five work and socializing with his married fraternity brothers and their wives, playing bridge or canasta, smoking and drinking beer on weekends.

We were like two of those large cardboard images you see today. Picture the husband: a twenty-five-year-old man holding a briefcase, wearing a suit and tie, a summer weave hat and horn-rimmed glasses. The wife is posed like a mannequin in a pink organdy apron and high heels, smiling, holding up a package of frozen spinach—look behind us, we're flat and empty.

In moments of quiet desperation, when my poster husband was out late, I sat on the sofa with floral slip covers, strumming my plastic baritone ukulele, singing "That'll be the Day," a Buddy Holly song.

Who am I, anyway? Oh, that's right, it's 1958 and I'm Betty Crocker living out the American Dream.

I trusted that my husband knew best because he was the man, so I deferred to him about everything. I wanted to believe in myself, too, but there was nothing to believe in now. I kept all my feelings buried.

Color me beige with a cardboard spine, easily blown away on any windy day. I had hit the PAUSE button of my life,

In a perspective drawing of the Self, this would be my vanishing point.

~

One hot Wednesday night in early September, after three months of marriage, we were lying in that bed with the squeaky springs, and I started crying and just couldn't stop. It was one of those unbelievable crying jags that started in one place and ended up in another, covering the entire three months of marriage. I fell apart.

He tried to comfort me.

What freaked me out the most was that a *veil* had lifted, and I had a moment of realization that neither my body nor my soul were mine any more.

They belonged to my husband.

I went into the living room and lay on the sofa and hugged the sofa cushion and kept on crying. Then I picked up my ukelele and strummed the chords to "Show Me the Way to Go Home."

I felt disappointed and guilty, as if I'd broken a contract I'd signed, but one in which I hadn't read the fine print. Part of me knew that all I had to do was just keep playing the part, like everyone else did, and it would all work out.

But it hadn't. It was broken, like that handprint I'd dropped on the sidewalk back in kindergarten. And it wasn't going to work out.

After that crying jag was over I announced the next morning that I was leaving.

Then it was all over.

I left it up to him and his Mother to take care of all the wedding gifts. I didn't care what they did with them.

All I remember was getting off the trolley at Holderness Street and walking in heels down that long block back into that awful, dark old house, the worse place of all. But at least I wouldn't have marriage responsibilities I couldn't possibly carry out.

The house was empty. Mother had taken a job as a housemother for the Georgia Baptist Children's Home. Mother and I didn't talk about the breakup except to acknowledge it over the phone.

I was all alone.

That's the problem with aspirations; if you don't reach the moon and stars, you have nowhere to fall but down. I had an awful sensation of falling backwards, down, down, down into misery and apprehension, as if I'd suddenly been left alone within the darkness of the sixth ring of Hell, except there was no friendly guide to help me up, and out.

Each morning I dragged myself out of bed and walked up Holderness Street to the bus stop, waiting in the dark, keeping my head down, not wanting to make eye contact with anyone, utterly ashamed to be back where I started. I was a failure with nothing to look forward to. It was good that it was dark though. I liked the dark better. No one would notice me. I was going through the motions of the day like some seedy B-movie in slow motion.

When I finally told the State Farm girls I'd left my husband, they were so kind and supportive. That was the first time I experienced sympathy. I'd been honest, a hard thing for me to do, to admit failure and be vulnerable.

It was good to have my job of answering the phone and take those wonderful coffee breaks—my only shred of happiness during that time. Ruth and Jan and I would walk to an old hotel in Decatur. It had a black-and-white tiled floor, a romantic lobby with potted palms, tall windows, and dark polished woodwork. The little dining room had linen napkins and served crispy cinnamon toast and coffee. At least I had that tiny oasis of beauty in a hotel lobby once a day during a coffee break in my otherwise miserable world.

~

I finally told Dorothy. Not long after that she called me.

"Chipper, Babe," she said. "Let's go over to Athens to see the University Theater production."

We rode the Greyhound bus because neither of us had a car. Monte had stayed on for graduate school and was in *Teahouse of the August Moon*.

It was good to be sitting back in the Fine Arts Auditorium, noticing the house lights dimming to a count of ten, then watching the curtain go up. It was a good and bad reminder of my last four years, juxtaposed to my current misery.

We got back to Atlanta late that night, and I had to take the night bus home. I sat there in the bus station after Dorothy left, afraid to smoke a cigarette, like I might look like a bus station slut or something. So I just sat there, not wanting to move, because the night bus went only as far as Lee Street, over a mile from my house.

I'd walked that dark mile once before barefoot, carrying my high heels and stockings tucked in my purse. That night Dorothy and I had gone to see Sylvia Sidney in the play *Auntie Mame*. We'd attended the late night reception and got to meet her, and that's when I found out the night bus stopped at Lee Street. It was awful to think of walking home that far again, down all those long blocks in the eerie darkness. I remembered the apprehension I felt between street lights. Block after block, alone. Another bad-dream movie coming true.

I couldn't imagine spending money for a taxi, so I kept sitting there in the bus station hoping I'd get the *wherewithal* to catch the bus. I could never ask for help, but this time I did. I called my estranged husband from a phone booth.

"Could you come and get me?" I said.

I guess he was waiting for that phone call because he was there at the bus station right away, being really nice. He drove me home, and we sat in his car talking in the darkness. He asked if I'd be willing to see a marriage counselor.

I felt better just asking for his help. He seemed so mature as if everything would be okay if I would just do what he suggested. He mentioned there was an office Christmas party coming up. When he said that, I thought of how much I'd messed up his career, running out on him like that.

Oh, Lord! What must everyone be thinking?

~

I remember that Christmas party, too. It felt weird to be dressing up again for a date in that old bedroom, putting on my black homecoming-dance dress with a white inset in the bodice, knowing my *husband* was picking me up. I leaned into those vanity mirrors, once again, carefully applying mascara, then using an eyelash curler, thinking I must play my role again as wife of an ambitious husband, anxious to show off his young spouse and make a good impression.

Places. Curtain time.

That was one swanky evening, too. Larry and I first had cocktails at his boss's house in Ansley Park. Then we rode in the backseat of their black '57 Cadillac with tail fins, as Len drove to downtown Atlanta. We went up an elevator and exited on the rooftop of the Atlanta Athletic Club.

It was exciting. I liked glamour. I needed the attention. Someone at the party brought me a 'Seven and Seven,' a drink I'd never heard of. I hated the taste of blended whiskey and didn't care for the salty mushy black eyes of caviar on the long candlelit rooftop buffet.

I kept smiling, sipping on the bourbon, looking appealingly naive, wearing black suede spike heels and a black dress with two crinolines underneath, coolly blowing out smoke from a Kent filtered cigarette, and especially remembering that Betty Crocker is never again allowed to scream.

MARRIAGE COUNSELING

I was scared to see a marriage counselor.

What would she ask me?

She probably had that list of *errors of my ways* my husband had written down on a sheet from a yellow legal pad.

"I'm Millie Keeler," she said with a smile. She was short and dumpy with dark curly hair. I followed behind her up the narrow stairs to a tiny office on the top floor of an old house. There was just enough room for her desk and a chair.

After one or two sessions, I found my hour spent with Mrs. Keeler a relief. She reminded me of Aunt Gladys with her sense of humor. She was interested in whatever I said. Soon she convinced me to give the marriage another try.

My husband found us another apartment. We had fun buying a Christmas tree together, giving each other presents, and taking a few pictures to remember our first Christmas, 1958.

On my last appointment in December, Mrs. Keeler said, "Charlotte, we think it best that you see a psychiatrist."

Oh, Lord, what is wrong with me? I wondered.

~

Chapter 20

"Vy Are You Here?"

"AND 'VY ARE YOU HERE?" asked a thin woman with a Viennese accent, as I cautiously slumped into the curved captain's chair by her desk. I scanned the dark paneled walls, yellow lamp, drawn drapes, wondering why she hadn't asked me to lie on the low psychiatrist's couch, like I'd seen in the movies.

I thought, *What a question, 'Vy are you here?' You're the psychiatrist. You should know!*

I'd had to ask off from work to come to downtown Atlanta for this terrifying appointment. I kept shading my eyes on the bus, glancing at buildings skidding by, noticing clusters of tired workers leaning on bus-stop poles. In windows on Peachtree Street, I saw dress shop mannequins posing mutely in white gloves, stylish hats, and dainty veils. The gray January sky and bus fumes gave me a headache. I kept wondering what the bus passengers would think if they knew I was going to see a psychiatrist. Maybe they'd get up and run, like I might go berserk or something.

I thought I'd gotten along famously with Mrs. Keeler at Family Counseling and that I'd made good progress, so much so, that recently I'd let myself get angry enough to throw a coffee cup across the kitchen at the cupboard door. I'd also found out I had a *clitoris*, thanks to a diagrammed sex pamphlet Mrs. Keeler had given me—though I was yet to know its purpose.

Vy am I here? . . . I don't know 'Vy-I-am-here.'

I had accepted this psychiatric referral without question or protest, like a mute bird with a furrowed brow. My task was to adjust. My husband wanted it. His parents wanted me to be the decent, loving, daughter-in-law they thought they were getting. Society wanted me to adjust.

I was not about to tell Dr. Karla Braun, with her horn-rimmed glasses and tight serious mouth, how ashamed I felt about having to see her, and that it had really hurt my feelings to lose jolly Mrs. Keeler, of all people.

I knew Mother would be ashamed if she knew her only child was seeing a psychiatrist. Didn't they always blame the Mother? More than that, I would be humiliated to think that any of my college friends might hear I'd gone *cuckoo*!

I already missed Mrs. Keeler's laugh and warm sparkling eyes. I'd never had anyone listen to me before. It wasn't fair. Just as I was almost happy—actually looking forward to going for my weekly counseling session—BOOM! The happiness carpet was pulled right out from under me.

Earlier, I'd gotten up enough nerve to ask my husband why I had to see a psychiatrist. He said anxiety and depression.

He knew best.

I was a compliant girdled and gloved girl of the 50s. It had not occurred to anyone, let alone me, that I might not want to be married.

Tiny pewter eyes peered at me through thick lenses.

"Vy do you 'sink you're here?" she asked again.

I scraped at a bloody piece of skin on my thumb, trying to think, but still nothing came to me. I fingered the bumpy brass upholstery tacks—a blind person seeking a secret Braille message for support.

"Mrs. Keeler said I was to come," I said dutifully.

I noticed the imposing walnut bookcase with intimidating psychiatric titles.

What if there really is something wrong with me?

All I knew was that I was twenty-two, having so-called "adjustment" problems. After two months of counseling the director had *first* informed my husband, not me, 'We recommend your wife receive further treatment.'

"Mrs. Keeler said you *vere* to come?" she repeated, rubbing a knobby wrist bone. It reminded me of the freaky wrist bone on Wanda Blalock who sat next to me in business math. In my opinion Wanda got way too much attention from that oddity.

"See, I left my husband after three months," I said, "but we're back together again, thanks to Mrs. Keeler."

I smiled, eyeing her for approval for the progress I'd already made.

None came.

I already knew in thirty seconds I'd *never* be able to talk to *her* like I did Mrs. Keeler. I'd never want to tell her about growing up in a dingy house, hating our grimy, dust-covered window sills, open shelves nailed to the walls, peeling wallpaper —and the loneliness.

For sure, I'd never want to tell her anything about Mother, either—not that there was really anything I blamed her for—but I didn't want any damned questions about '*your Mother*' to catch me off guard.

My hands were freezing and my feet, too. Everything about that dark paneled tomb was chilly. I heard a mechanical click of an electric heater underneath her desk. She scribbled notes on a yellow pad. (*Another yellow pad!*) Notes about me. Secret impressions. Thoughts I knew she would never share with me. I was scared as if this time I might really be injected with truth serum."

~

After three months of getting nowhere fast, I kept repeating things like feeling guilty about smoking and drinking, because it was a sin.

"Vhat do *you* 'sink?" she'd ask.

No matter what I said, she would ask me back a question, and I didn't *ever* have a decent answer. Oh, Lord, I just didn't know. I didn't know anything, apparently, and I was getting a little fed up, too.

~

In our first session in April, Dr. Braun was sporting a new frizzled hair style. She stared at me silently, as usual, waiting for me to begin. I knew the routine now. She had a fresh page of her yellow pad out, pencil sharpened. Today her hair reminded me of this one really bad *Toni* home perm Mother had experimented on with me. Mine turned out awful. I wondered where Dr. Braun lived and what kind of car she drove. *Maybe a Volvo.* I had looked her name up in the phone book. She lived in Sandy Springs.

I came in feeling good, since I was getting used to the routine, because sometimes I *did* talk, but just odds and ends about work and cooking. But then I glanced at her bookshelf and saw part of a book title " . . . *and Other Character Disorders,"* and that turned me from blasé to anxious again.

Stop that. Betty Crocker is not allowed to scream! That's what got you here in the first place. Think of something fun, pleasant, a good story. What would she want to hear? No. What would I *want to tell, is a better question.*

"I could tell you about Robert, my grammar school boyfriend," I said smiling, trying to make myself happy.

"Robert?" she asked.

"Yeah, we played a song flute duet together. Do you know what a song flute is?"

Did she nod or not? I thought I should explain since she had that foreign accent.

"A song flute isn't like a real flute. It's made of plastic."

I waited for her response. *Nothing.* I think she had some kind of hard-and-fast non-disclosure rule.

"Go on," she said.

"Anyway, I really liked Robert . . . see, he played the trombone, and his Mother dressed him in these nice sweater vests, and we learned to do ballroom dancing together, and the fox trot, too. Did you have dancing in your grammar school?"

She raised her eyebrows ever so slightly.

Was that a yes or no? I couldn't tell.

"Continue," she said.

"See, I liked Robert because he was smart . . ."

And then I continued, rattling on and on. She looked so bored, so then I decided to skip to a good part, something I'd actually been wanting to tell somebody.

"See, we usta to hold hands during the classroom movies. He ran the movie projector and I turned off the lights. We sat on the back row. Our teacher left us in charge. We felt pretty grown up, and all, y'know, it was exciting, like it was kind of illicit, if you know what I mean. Did you have movies in school when you were little?"

"No, ve didn't."

Yay! One point for me!

"Our time *eez* up."

~

The next appointment Dr. Braun was wearing a dark gray cardigan sweater, a gray tweed skirt, and soft white blouse with round pearl buttons. Pretty classy stuff. Her perm had calmed down some, too.

"You *vere* telling me about Robert."

Alright! We were finally on the same page. I had looked forward to finishing my story about holding hands during those movies. It was a good Hollywood story to me.

"Well, we had these Encyclopedia Britannica films every Friday, and one cartoon. Mrs. Gilmer, our teacher, let me fill out the rental forms, y'know, so I knew what the films were going to be. The class would shout, 'What's the cartoon, Charlotte? What's the cartoon?' See, we had this one cartoon about bees bombarding each other, zooming back and forth to the music of "The Flight of the Bumble Bee.""

I waved my arms in the air, imitating the bees and humming a bit of the fast melody.

"Oh, we loved that cartoon, and the class cheered when they saw the title."

I noticed Dr. Braun wasn't taking any notes. I fingered my chewed-up nails, knowing—yet, not knowing—why I was rattling on about zooming bees, and what it had felt like to be chosen by both Robert and Mrs. Gilmer.

I wanted Dr. Braun to think I was special, too. At the least, I deserved a laugh. *Damn*!

She rubbed the back of her neck. I wondered if she was tired. My appointments were at four. *Who else has she seen today*, I wondered, *deranged bankers, impotent writers, other depressed young girls, like me?*

I launched back in. "Then in sixth grade, Mrs. Gilmer chose Robert and me for the king and queen of hearts. Let me tell you, it was a *big* production, on the school auditorium stage, and, *listen*, when you're eleven years old, that is a big deal! I guess that's how I came to major in drama, y'know. I never wanted to be an actress, though, just a star."

Dr. Braun touched two thin fingers to her mouth to stifle a yawn. She still hadn't taken any notes.

I looked *right at* Dr. Braun and slowed down my story.

"So . . . this *one* Saturday at the movies . . . I got really *brave* and put my arm on the back of the seat around Robert's shoulder. It was a daring thing to do, but I just couldn't help myself. I felt so close to him and I'd never . . . I'd never had feelings like that before."

I could hear my voice change from breezy to serious and a little emotional, which surprised and scared me to hear myself say '*I felt so close to him*' out loud, but I was in the middle of such a good story.

"See," I said, leaning forward, "Even though he was a boy, he was an only child, *too*. I wanted to show him my feelings. I knew how he felt, *inside*."

I shifted gears, catching myself from tapping into a place I didn't want to go.

"But, guess what?" I fairly shouted. "The next Monday, this girl came up to me in the girls' bathroom and asked if I'd really put my arm around Robert at the movies. Then somebody else chimed in and said that girls weren't supposed to do that kind of thing, and after that, I was ashamed and felt like some hussy in the movies."

I sat back in my chair, relieved that it felt so good to be telling her that story, since I'd never told anyone, and it'd been bugging me, and I wasn't so sure that it didn't have something to do with the real reason I was there.

Inside I could still feel tension from telling and re-living how it felt to hear gossip and criticism, as if my insides were about to break up, about to come unglued just from telling her.

Dr. Braun eased the bottom of the yellow pad off her desk, slanting it out of my view, then she casually leaned back and began to take notes.

Did she think I didn't see that! What is she writing? Aggressive sexual tendencies at eleven. Disgusting! Harlot. Charlotte-the-Harlot!! Just as a joke to herself. Oh, I just wish I had enough nerve to ask her, "Dr. Braun, WHAT did you just write down about me?"

"None of your business," she'd say coolly.

"What do you mean, NONE of my business? It's MY guts I'm spilling out here!"

Then I pictured myself jumping up, like in a movie, and wrestling the yellow pad from her bony fingers, only to discover she'd scribbled arrows, tic-tac-toe squares, and other doodles. Victorious, she would laugh raucously, throwing herself backwards, hysterically falling out of her swivel-chair onto her silent gray carpet. And I would laugh, too, just seeing her laugh, since she had never once cracked a smile in four months of therapy.

But instead, I put on another dramatic voice.

"And in that *same* girls' bathroom, a girl named Anne said, 'Robert likes Judith Foster better than yo-oo-u.'"

I looked at Dr. Braun and actually asked a question, "How come girls do that? I hate that kind of snippy gossip!"

"Vhat do *you* 'sink?" She barely raised an eyebrow.

I hated it when she asked me a question back. I didn't VAHNT to 'SINK.

"I don't *know!*" I snapped with annoyance, clutching the leather chair arms, jamming my stockinged feet up under the chair. And I actually saw her lip twitch a bit, like, *now we're getting somewhere.*

I was surprised and embarrassed to hear myself tell my corny story of heartbreak with Robert that I'd carried around for ten years. I stopped talking and just sat there.

'Clamming up,' Mother would've called it.

I wanted Dr. Braun to *like* me. I wanted her to show some warmth and caring—laugh at my jokes, at least, so I could pour out whatever it was I needed to say.

She doesn't even care! I thought. *She never tells me anything about herself. I'm twenty-two, for God's sake! I should have gotten over that, by now!*

Didn't she know that just one little approving smile could relieve all those feelings that seemed to poison me and make me aloof and anxious?

"Our time *eez* up."

In the next session, when she opened the door, Dr. Braun touched me gently on the shoulder as she ushered me into her dark-night-of-the-soul office. I shrank away as if I'd been bitten by a viper and moved as far away as I could, heading over to the herringbone psychiatrist couch and lay down. I'd always wanted to try it out and was surprised at how stiff and unforgiving it felt with no springs underneath. I didn't speak the entire time, clammed up with fear of exposing myself in some reckless way.

I mumbled a quick defensive "nuh-unh" in response to the intimidating question of asking me if my *silence* was about her touching me as I entered.

"And, how *did* that make you feel?"

She had cut me to the quick. I felt tears brimming, gritted my teeth and closed my eyes to hold myself together.

I wasn't about to tell her things I didn't even let myself know.

It's hard to describe what it feels like to deny feelings. I wanted to let myself dissolve away in tears and clear out my lungs and throat, and loosen the tension in every cell in my body for never being able to say, *"Help me. Hold me. Love me. Please don't leave me."* I'd learned to avert all those slings and arrows with a nonchalant smile and a carefully built shield of cardboard and shame, glossed over with something artificially bright, like my fake Pepsodent smile.

That day I held back tears because I couldn't say, "I need you to like me, to understand me, and maybe even to love me."

I was such a good little girl warrior, joking, entertaining, keeping up a good front, keeping my heart protected, so it wouldn't break into a million little pieces.

That day on the stony herringbone couch, I forced back sobs that wanted to burst up my throat where every flaw and secret shame was hidden. I didn't know how much I needed tender loving care until I was caught off guard by the touch on the shoulder from a psychiatrist.

"Our time *eez* up," said Dr. Braun.

My fifty minutes of shame was up.

I rose from the hard couch.

I'd acted like a silent fool and wasted her time and mine. I hated myself because I felt like I'd lost and she'd won. And I hated her for having that kind of callous power.

That was my last visit.

As I left her office, I felt so hopeless that late afternoon, walking back down the narrow sloping sidewalk to the bus stop, so glad to be out of there—glad to be away from that awful house on Holderness Street, too, but marriage wasn't where I wanted to be, either. I thought of the title of a book I used to see in the school library, *Nobody's Child*, one I'd never even wanted to pick up to browse.

My wedding vows were like terms of imprisonment, but I knew I would honor them, because I was a girdled and gloved girl of the 50s with nowhere else to go, and I was pretty sure I was pregnant.

~ ~ ~

EPILOGUE

Epilogue

From Radio to YouTube

> *"In the world of my dreams,*
> *we'd all be understood."*
>
> — lyrics by Chip McDaniel
> from *Silent Dreams:The Musical*

IN 1974 AFTER STRUGGLING THROUGH sixteen years of marriage with one husband, one bathroom, three sons, and eight dogs, I was back sleeping in a single bed in Athens, Georgia—in a little brick house I've lived in for nearly fifty years.

I'd failed marriage, too.

I was a soccer mom, a Little League mom, driving a faded aqua Impala station wagon, buying baseball gloves and cleats, cooking up stacks of pancakes, pots of spaghetti, turkey tetrazinni, and reading books to the boys, like *To Kill a Mockingbird*, *Lord of the Flies*, and *The Princess Bride*.

Little miracles began to happen after the divorce. I no longer bit my nails. My rheumatoid arthritis cleared up. I bought a piano and taught myself some jazz chords, and for two weekends I was happy to play piano at Sparky's, a local seafood restaurant.

I needed to earn money, so at forty I scrambled up a Fortune 500 ladder from mailroom to corporate communications.

Bought a leather briefcase.

Dressed for success.

I even flew on a Lear Jet from Athens, Ga. to Jefferson City, sitting behind the pilots, seeing the altimeter climb to 20,000.

I am woman, hear me roar! From streetcars to Lear Jets!

~

In the meantime, on my fiftieth birthday I visited Mother at her nursing home, thinking about my own mortality. She was sitting in a tan recliner, her shiny red diabetic legs propped up.

Mother was glad to see me and fished a notepad from the wide pocket of her sleeveless cotton print dress. On the pocket were embroidered initials, M.A.D. for Margaret Ashurst DeLoach, her third husband's last name.

"Shug, listen to what I wrote today!"

She read, "How would you like to be the first member of the Crazy Club?"

Before I could reply, she said, "You *can't*, I'M the first member!!"

We laughed together.

She continued, "In twenty-five words or less, tell me why you think I'm crazy."

Again, before I could remark, she said, "Thank you, I'm now President!"

We laughed again, then our conversation meandered, and suddenly I heard myself say, "You know, Mother, I think you were the perfect Mother for me," and as I said it, I burst into tears and fell to my knees with years of bottled up emotion.

"I don't know how to help you," I said, "tell me what to do."

I put my head in her lap, sobbing as I'd never done before. My heart broke open with remorse. Tears soaked into her thin sleeveless print dress. I felt the passive purr of her breathing, the warmth of her thigh and her familiar Mother smell underneath talcum powder.

She didn't comfort me, nor cry herself, nor caress me. I wanted her to put her arthritic hand on my head, like Jesus, and absolve me of my suffering, saying, *'Go child, live your life. You deserve it. I want you to! It's O.K. I'll tough it out.'* My hand rested on the dry skin of her bare arm, and that seemed to be enough contact for us.

Finally, she said, "You can be a member of the Crazy Club!"

Startled, I looked up at her tired old green eyes as she smiled a toothless grin and we both laughed, and it seemed just like old times. And now I'm *so* glad I said that to Mother, and that she heard it. I think about that all the time now, and I'm still surprised that I *meant it* when I said she was *the perfect mother for me*. I've come to realize that uttering those words was a moment of grace. And you don't get many of those.

She died on my birthday in 1991.

I had a private memorial service for her with her grandsons and a few people who knew her. After sharing some stories I said to the group, "When Mother was sixty, she got a tape recorder. One day she made a broadcast to entertain her unseen audience with a few songs, some poems and her clocks chiming. I can't think of a better tribute to Mother than to have her perform at her own funeral."

And I pressed *PLAY.*

WHAT IS THE MEANING OF LIFE?

As I turned fifty, I believed my lifeline indicated I was going to die at fifty-five. The sons were off to seek their fortunes, so I raised the lid on a steel gray coffin and sleeping beauty walked out that corporate door.

I have come to know that that fear of death was coming from my instinctual self—that wise intuiting woman in the *knowing cave*. I was right to have heeded. Gradually I relaxed, and began to sense the rest of my life on the tip of my tongue, so to speak.

I felt my life had five distinct parts and that the last part would be the best, if only I could manage to get there and discover what was around that last bend.

On the first Monday of retirement, I took my coffee out on the deck, listening to the birds' chirp, hearing the distant hum of morning traffic, and pondered.

What is the meaning of my life?

I knew I needed the freedom to create a lifestyle that was perfect for me. I was pretty sure I could live off my savings if I was careful. Then I simply followed my bliss. I started a garden. I went to the library and read wherever my interests took me: Katherine Mansfield's and Anais Nin's journals, Thomas Hardy's *Jude the Obscure,* Theodore Dreiser's *An American Tragedy* and *Sister Carrie,* Dostoyevski's *Crime and Punishment, Angela's Ashes* by Frank McCourt.

I began a journal. I started a memoir called *Shug*.

They say you can't go home again. *My God!* I couldn't ever *leave* home. Those hungry ghosts from the past gnawed away.

Over the twenty-five years I've been writing this memoir, I've come to discover that each memory had layers of meanings, at first personal, then universal.

Music was the connective tissue between dreams and reality.

When I finally got a keyboard that recorded music, it changed my life. Now when I hear the piano solo of "Yesterday's Love," I'm that restless, lonely teenager on a hot summer day, sitting at an upright piano, creating something beautiful—and eternal. Late one night I was tired of recording do-overs, so I took a break and absent-mindedly played five perfect notes:

Hold - on - to - your - dreams

I heard the notes and the words both, like I had with "Yesterday's Love." The words had been in my head from reading a book, *The Cry For Myth* by Rollo May.

Hold on to your dreams.
Keep them in a special place.
Great or small,
they sometimes may take years
or a life - time!

Yes, a lifetime, indeed. Time and the century were running out. My lyrics continued:

> **And if you are not a great exception, yourself,**
> **well, then be a small one, at least,**
> **that your efforts may inspire others as well.**

I loved that song so much. Suddenly, I *knew* I was born to write a musical. I felt I had a second chance to make something of my life—my own *deus ex machina!*

I set it in New York in 1955 where I'd wanted to go after college. I created characters out of the past. I gave Mother the role of Vera, who played piano for the Silent Movies. I made my grandmother into Mrs. Chap, the owner of a boarding house/Hotel Chappelear, where Vera lives.

I designed a coffee house cafe across the street from the boarding house. Chez Coffeé.

I created an alter-ego, young songwriter Augie. In the opening scene he sings:

> **I want to be somebody, someone debonnaire**
> **Not lost in a crowd, someone with a flair,**
> **Someplace I belong, who will hear my song?**
> **I hope it's soon.**

When Vera dies, her diary reveals an affair with Silent Movie idol, Fernando Vega. Augie then writes songs for a new musical, *Silent Lovers*. Because of wanting *my father* to come *see me backstage*, I wrote that scene for Augie. After opening night Augie breaks down in tears telling the audience that his father came backstage to see him. Then he sings:

> **I've waited so long for this day**
> **It seemed so far away**
> **I've found a place where I belong**
> **Someone to hear my song**
> **Someone to hear my song.**

I called the musical, *Silent Dreams*. It ends with a finale, "The Great Circle of Love." I loved every struggling minute of giving birth to the story and the songs. I gave it my best shot to get it produced, but I never connected with the right people.

This time *I'd failed myself*. It was depressing.

~

Up until the *last* revisions of this memoir, I thought that if I ever got to Heaven, the last person I'd want to find would be my grandmother. I had nothing to say to her. *Nothing*.

After many rewrites—holding her in my hands, so to speak—I came to see my grandmother's life differently.

I never thought I'd say this, but now I'd go find Grandma and drop to my knees and tell her how sorry I was to have been such a burden. I'd tell Grandma I hadn't realized how I had ruined her life for the thirteen years she had to take care of me.

Also, all these years I said I'd *never, ever* use my maiden name, *Ashurst*. I rationalized that I could have a little poetic justice by withholding my father's name. But now I see that my father gave me my curiosity about words and maybe a few points in I.Q. He sent those monthly checks, so I've added my maiden name as part of the author name.

FROM RADIO TO YOUTUBE

The radio was still a comfort, living alone, at seventy-three, so I kept it on at night. In January, 2010, at 3 a.m., I couldn't sleep and heard about a contest on BBC World News:

"Send us a two-minute video to the *BBC My World* contest," said an enthusiastic British announcer.

I could never resist a contest!

Social Security was coming in now. I'd bought a MacBook, and had just learned to make a music video, using old photos and the song, "Hold On to Your Dreams."

What timing!

The next morning I figured out how to upload it to the BBC. Then I received a BBC email asking me to cut twenty seconds.

I wasn't sure if I could.

The next day I got a phone call.

A very British male voice said, "I'm the producer for the *BBC My World* project."

The BBC is calling me! I must be dreaming, I thought.

"Have you considered narrating your film?" he asked.

"Narrating?" I said.

"Yes, your own voice would lend much," he said.

"I don't know. I could try," I said hesitantly.

"We liked your little film very much," he said and hung up.

I was ecstatic. *"Film,"* he'd called it. I was shaking.

What a task, writing out my *entire life* in two minutes.

Lord! Here I was, making a real movie, something I'd always wanted to do, fitting it all together in *i-movie* with my own music, narration and photos. I'm telling you, those were the happiest weeks of my ENTIRE LIFE! Someone of note *cared* about something I was working on after all these years. I was doing work I loved and learning how to get better, still hoping I'd be discovered as some talented little genius from the "sticks" in Georgia. The narration begins . . .

Welcome to my world of silent dreams.
I was an only child with no daddy,
so writing songs for me has always been
about being born with a broken heart.
I know it's hard to think that a baby
could come out of a womb so sad and all, but I did.
Mother loved the movies, posed me for photos,
so I wanted to be a movie star.
I thought maybe I'd be so famous
one day my father would come and meet me or something,
so I majored in drama.
But that didn't go anywhere.
So I got married, raised a family.
Then I tried to play jazz piano.
Now, fast forward a lotta years
to when I get a keyboard and write this song:

Hold On To Your Dreams.
It's so beautiful I write an entire musical around it,
set it in New York where I wanted to go after college.
I called it Silent Dreams,
but it never got anywhere, either.
So now I live in a little world of my own creation,
put up old movie star photos like I had when I was little,
sketch in a journal, have a secret garden,
dress up, take photos, and I always have the music
and that's enough.

~

My little film made the *short list* of entries from the Americas, and was posted to *BBC My World Feb. 23, 2010.*

I emailed the BBC once more to ask how long the video could be viewed. Apparently it was to remain in their BBC archives. *Hoo-ray!* Now I can rest in peace envisioning Mother and me—and the music—together forever.

Better than a tombstone!

Yes, writing, creating music, and dreamwork helped me sort out and understand how my early years influenced my life's journey. I created my own meaning as I went along, turning sadness into another song "Morning Tears." I even made a CD of a few piano solos, including, "Yesterday's Love."

Maybe writing this *memoir* has been about reconciliation, redemption, and salvation, but I think my *life* has really been about learning to love my fate. *Amor fati.* So that, at best, I might have that "Hollywood happy ending" I longed for—for I do have a measure of peace from the grace that has come from understanding and accepting the past.

~ ~ ~

Amor Fati

Love your fate
even if you didn't get what you wanted,
even if you didn't want what you got,
even if your plans were thwarted,
and ended in dead end streets,
even if hope was overrated,
even if the prison bars,
were of your own making.

Love it because
the sun will be there every day
even when you can't see it,
because being human *itself* is beautiful,
in some strange mad way.

~

ABOUT THE AUTHOR

Charlotte (*Chip*) Ashurst McDaniel
holds a BFA in Drama.
She is a self-taught musician, songwriter,
composer, photographer, graphic artist, and poet.
She is currently writing
Confessions of a Blue Tomato.

. . . *stay tuned*

http://www.bbc.co.uk/worldservice/arts/
2010/02/100223_chips_myworld.shtml

(The BBC Archives Link)

*A music video **YouTube/Girdled and Gloved**, shows additional
photos with "Yesterday's Love" as background music.
Music video **YouTube/Hold On To Your Dreams**
Music video **YouTube/Remembering Sandra Brown**
email: janamedrova @ yahoo.com*